# Smoothies & Juices

# Smoothies & Juices

## 365 delicious and nutritious blends

Natalie Savona

METRO BOOKS
New York

**METRO BOOKS**
New York

An Imprint of Sterling Publishing
387 Park Avenue South
New York, NY 10016

METRO BOOKS and the distinctive Metro Books logo
are trademarks of Sterling Publishing Co., Inc.

Managing Editor: Judy Barratt
Editor: Rebecca Miles
Managing Designer: Manisha Patel
Designer: Allan Sommerville
Commissioned Photography: William Lingwood
Stylists: David Morgan (food) and Helen Trent

Juicer supplied by Theolife Ltd: Samson 6 in 1
Multipurpose Juice Extractor GB9001
www.samsonjuicer.co.uk

ISBN: 978-1-4351-3259-7

For information about custom editions, special sales, and premium
and corporate purchases, please contact Sterling Special Sales at
800-805-5489 or specialsales@sterlingpublishing.com.

Manufactured in China

10 9 8 7 6 5 4 3 2

www.sterlingpublishing.com

**Notes**
None of the information in this book is meant as a
substitute for professional medical advice. If you are
in any doubt as to the suitability of any of the
therapeutic methods or recipes given in this book,
consult your doctor.

Follow either the imperial or the metric measurements
when making the recipes. The measurements are not
interchangeable.

# contents

# introduction

The mouthwatering tang of freshly squeezed orange juice straight from squeezer to mouth within minutes – my early experiences of fresh juice was, as for most of us, from this staple citrus fruit. My first venture into the more alien world of vegetable juices came on a beach in Thailand – a large glass of frothy, deep orange carrot juice. This sublime taste in an exotic location marked the beginning of a culinary adventure.

First, using a basic, modestly-priced juicer salvaged from the depths of my parents' kitchen, I turned out concoctions of almost anything I had in the fruit bowl or refrigerator. As I became bolder, I requested an expensive, high-powered juicer as a present a few years ago and haven't looked back since.

The overriding selling point for all juices and smoothies is that they attain the magical quality, so elusive in so much of what we eat and drink today, of tasting sensational *and* being supremely good for you. Raw fruit and vegetables are laden with vitamins, minerals, enzymes and other ingredients that give us a boost in energy, help ward off illness and keep our bodies' cleansing processes working optimally.

Once you have developed the habit of making your own fresh juice combinations each morning, nothing else will do. I wager you will become so convinced that you would no sooner go without your daily juice than without brushing your teeth. Ahead of you are recipes for more juices and smoothies than you could ever ask for, not to mention a selection of frozen drinks and some refreshing teas. My breakfast is regularly fresh, home-made juice and a creamy smoothie. You really couldn't get a much better start to the day.

## how to use this book

This book provides you with 365 recipes to guide and inspire you to begin a daily juicing habit. It is organized into chapters of juices, smoothies and quenchers, each with its own coloured thumb tab for quick and easy reference. In addition, the tabs in chapters 2 and 3 ("making juices" and "making smoothies") show different fruit and vegetable icons denoting the prime ingredient around which a group of recipes is based. For example, a pear on a blue (juice) tab indicates a page of pear-based juice recipes, and a mango on a pink (smoothie) tab indicates mango-based smoothie recipes. In turn, these icons are used on yellow tabs in the ingredients lists in chapter 1. This handy tabbing system will allow you to choose recipes with ease, according to preference or what is in your refrigerator.

For further information on their specific health benefits, the recipes also list the main vitamins, minerals and other key nutrients in each drink. In addition, each recipe has a star-rating system giving the drink marks out of five for its energy-boosting, detoxing and immunity-boosting properties, and its benefits to the digestive system and the skin. At the end of the book, there is a nutrient chart providing further information on vitamins and minerals, and an ailments chart with suggested juices and smoothies to drink to help combat a range of common illnesses.

# juicing
# basics

## chapter 1

You're sold on the idea that juicing is a good thing: you know that fresh juices are not only delicious but also packed with healthy ingredients. But before you go rushing out to buy a state-of-the-art juicer, take some time to absorb the advice presented in this chapter. This will help you get the most out of your juicing.

Over the following pages we look at the different kinds of juice drinks you can make and offer some suggestions on the basic kit you'll need. We explore why juices really are so good for you – we examine the many benefits of drinking juice daily and reveal how the body uses this direct source of nutrients for optimum health. We discover that there are few fruit and vegetables that cannot be consumed in the form of a nutritious drink, and learn how best to choose and prepare them. Finally, we look at some of the optional extras, such as flaxseeds and wheatgerm, that can add a healthy bonus to your glass.

# why juice?

First of all, let us not forget that one of the most important aspects of anything we eat or drink is pleasure. Savouring a home-made, fresh juice is, for anyone who has tried it, an immensely pleasurable experience. Not only does it taste truly delicious, it also invigorates your body and mind, and gives the added satisfaction of having created it yourself.

Following on from the pleasure principle comes the effect that food and drink has on our body and mind. Raw, fresh juice is probably one of the most health-affirming, rejuvenating substances we can take. Drinking a fresh juice provides the body with nutrients on a superhighway – it's a fast delivery of vitamins, minerals, enzymes, carbohydrates, chlorophyll and countless other phytonutrients (nutrients derived from plants), which increasingly are being shown to boost health. And all of this contained in pure, fresh water. These natural blends of nutrients work together to enhance immunity, protecting us from not just colds and coughs but cancer and cardiovascular disease. Juices are powerhouses of antioxidants – nutrients such as vitamins A, C and E that fight oxidants (sometimes called free radicals) in our bodies which contribute to cancer, heart disease and aging. Other substances present in a juice, such as green chlorophyll, are particularly cleansing.

Even the least health-conscious person is now aware that we are supposed to have at least five servings of fruit and vegetables a day. Officially, a glass of juice counts a single portion, although immediately I'd say that a fresh, unadulterated, home-made juice, drunk straight from the jug, easily rates higher than your average shop-bought juice. A fresh juice also delivers the nutrients straight into your body within minutes, as it does not need to be digested in the way that fruit and vegetables do. And, given that some of your fruit, and probably all of your vegetables, are eaten at the same time as other foods, they are digested pretty slowly, and perhaps not too efficiently, so the nutrients may not be well absorbed.

So, in drinking your daily juice, you are not only fuelling yourself with energy, but you are also supporting your body's natural cleansing processes and helping stave off all manner of diseases. A home-made juice stands in a league of its own compared with off-the-shelf processed juices, not to mention coffee, tea, cordials, fizzy and so-called "energy" drinks, and is simply the best liquid refreshment that a body can have.

## juice or smoothie?

So, what is the difference? It's really a question of semantics – you can call your juice drinks what you like but for the sake of clarity, I have chosen to make a distinction. Simply, a juice is a drink made using a special juice extractor or citrus press and a smoothie is a drink made by mixing whole ingredients into a pulp in a blender. This book divides smoothies into two basic categories – fruity and creamy – where a creamy smoothie has a richer, creamier texture owing to the addition of yogurt to the mix. Some further variations on the smoothie theme appear in Chapter 4, Making Quenchers. Here, frozen fruit, ice and sparkling water are added for an extra-chilled, refreshing taste.

Now that we've got the semantics clear, there is actually a great deal of difference in the consistency and properties of the end products. With a juice you are getting just that – the juice from the fruit or vegetable as it is pushed through the extractor or press and the fibre is left behind. Because a smoothie is made by simply blending the fruit to a pulp, you get the whole fruit, including the fibre, merely in a different form. A smoothie can be breakfast in itself; a juice may be just the first course.

There are particular benefits associated with both the juice and the smoothie group of drinks. Juices provide nutrients at top speed – our bodies absorb their goodness with maximum efficiency, unhindered by any need to break down and digest bulkier foodstuffs. The lack of any fibre (left behind in the juicing process) means that our bodies can assimilate the nutrients from a juice in a matter of minutes rather than hours.

This is a sure-fire way of getting the most out of the vitamins, minerals, enzymes, cleansing elements and other nutritional goodness from a fruit or vegetable. After drinking a fresh juice, you feel invigorated almost immediately. By doing this daily, you provide your body with a high dose of naturally derived nutrients that boosts your health and helps keep you well-protected against toxins and disease.

Unlike juices, smoothies contain a good amount of fibre, something that is an important nutrient in itself. Indeed, fibre is an essential and all-too-often lacking ingredient in our diets. Not only does it help keep our guts moving, but it also helps them to keep healthy and to maintain the right levels of good bacteria. In addition to this, any drink using yogurt or milk, such as our creamy smoothies, becomes an important source of protein, another essential in a healthy diet.

## getting ready

### equipment

To make a variety of the recipes from this book, you will need a juice extractor, a citrus press and a blender. All of the juice recipes can be made using a juice extractor alone, although citrus fruits are best squeezed on a proper citrus press; they tend to clog up a juicer and leave behind a lot of their precious juice. For the purposes of this book, when I say "juice" a piece of fruit, I mean put it into an electric juicer, and when I say "squeeze" a fruit, I mean extract its juice by squeezing it on a citrus press.

When choosing your first juicer, buy one one at the lower end of the price range which will give you a perfectly good introduction to the joy of juicing. Most juicers are what are called "centrifugal extractors", which means they grate the fruit and quickly spin it out toward a mesh which catches the pulp and sends the juice down into a jug. This can make quite a mess in the machine and I suggest cleaning it immediately, before you've even allowed yourself a sip of the end product. It really doesn't take more than a couple of minutes.

Once you are converted to the delights and blessings of daily juicing, you may want to invest in one of the more expensive machines. Like with most things in life, you tend to get what you pay for – the more expensive juicers are likely to have a hardier motor and extract more juice per piece of fruit.

Citrus presses can be bought for a reasonable price in most kitchen accessory shops or department stores. They usually take the form of a stainless steel structure around which you squeeze halved fruit, although electric ones are also available.

The essential piece of smoothie kit is a blender. Most kitchens have one, albeit maybe little-used, but, again, you can buy one quite cheaply and it can soon become a smoothie-making machine creating breakfast or a refreshing drink in a flash.

## storing juices and smoothies

In my book, there really is no such thing as storing a juice or smoothie – you can't beat drinking them the moment you've made them. However, you may like to take them out to work or on a picnic. In that case, the best way to store them is to put a teaspoon of vitamin C powder or a squeeze of lemon juice in the bottom of the jug attached to the juicer. The vitamin C acts as an antioxidant, preventing the juice from turning brown. The same goes for smoothies. Also, keep the drinks covered and cool – in a sealed container in the refrigerator, or in a thermos flask.

# the ingredients

## choosing the best

Where possible, always choose fresh, local, organic produce that is in season. Organic fruits and vegetables provide you with all the goodness you need and none of the agrochemicals you don't. Also, buying locally supports your local economy and avoids adding to the economic and environmental costs of long-distance transport and storage of goods. (That said, you sometimes can't beat a delicious tropical mango or pineapple that has come all the way from India or Thailand!)

The following pages list information and preparation details for the fruits and vegetables used in the recipes (the foods follow the order of first appearance in the book). They are listed individually or in groups according to the batches of recipes within each chapter, and given a pictorial tab for easy reference.

## fruits

**Apple** — The best apples for juices and smoothies are sharp, crisp ones such as Granny Smith, Braeburn, Egremont Russet or Discovery. Apples make a fantastic base juice and are laden with health properties from their vitamin, mineral, malic acid and fibre content. They are not only detoxifying but also good for lowering cholesterol, aiding digestion and improving the condition of the skin. *Preparation: Wash well. For juicing, simply remove stalk and cut into pieces small enough to fit through your juicer. For smoothies, core and chop.*

**Grapefruit** — The sharp flavour of even the sweetest grapefruit is remarkably refreshing. White, pink, red is the order of increasing sweetness. Like all citrus fruits, grapefruits are packed with vitamin C, so good for immunity. The pith contains the bioflavonoids (powerful antioxidants which work alongside vitamin C), so don't peel that off when juicing grapefruits. However, squeezing the fruit using a citrus press actually produces more juice, but you lose the bioflavanoids. *Preparation: If juicing, peel and cut to fit. If squeezing, cut in half.*

**Orange** — The classic fruit juice, and of course the best way to get the most out of the fruit is to cut into quarters, suck out the juice and nibble the flesh from the skin. However, you simply can't beat fresh, home-made orange juice. Oranges, with their high vitamin C and bioflavonoid content are the famous immune-booster, but they are also rich in minerals and very cleansing. You get the most juice by squeezing them, but juicing means you also benefit from the bioflavonoids in the pith. *Preparation: If juicing, peel and chop into chunks. If squeezing, cut in half.*

**Raspberry** — Plump, summer raspberries may warrant popping into the mouth as is, but they do make a wonderful addition to a juice or blended drink. Like all berries, they are a rich source of nutrients, especially antioxidants. (This tab is used in the juice chapter only.) *Preparation: Wash well. Pick out any that are mouldy or still attached to the hulls.*

**Peach**, **nectarine** and **apricot** are from the same botanical family and their drinks appear in the book under the same pictorial tab.

> **Peach** — Good peaches yield a fantastic, rich nectar, ideal for blended drinks. Because of their high beta-carotene content, peaches help protect against lung, skin and digestive problems. With countless varieties of colour, it's best to choose a peach by its tenderness and its smell. A good peach will yield to a gentle squeeze and have a sweet scent, but an under-ripe specimen will be hard and barely smell of anything. *Preparation: Wash well. Halve, remove stone and chop into chunks.*
>
> **Nectarine** — The bald relative of peaches, good nectarines also burst with an orange, sweet nectar. They are a rich source of beta-carotene, as well as vitamin C and a spectrum of minerals. Use only when they are tender to a gentle squeeze in the palm. *Preparation: Wash well. Halve, remove stone and chop into chunks.*

**Apricot** — You're likely to get sweeter apricots in mid- and late-summer rather than earlier in the year. Choose them slightly soft to the touch and smelling sweet as they're unlikely to ripen further. Also, the riper they are, the higher their beta-carotene content. As a winter alternative soaked, dried apricots make a delicious, sweet addition to a smoothie. *Preparation (fresh apricots): Wash well. Halve and remove stone.*

**Cherry** — A luxury inasmuch as you need time and patience to yield a decent quantity of stoned, fresh fruit. But you will be grateful not only for the intense flavour of the juice: cherries contain rich antioxidant nutrients as well as highly alkaline properties, particularly good for arthritis and gout. *Preparation: Wash well. Slice in half and prise out the stone or use an olive stoner.*

**Pear** — As with many fruits, I hesitate to hand ripe Williams pears to my juicer rather than eat them straight up. While a juicy, ripe pear is best for blending, use a slightly under-ripe pear for juicing, even Comice or Conference varieties, and you will get a surprisingly thick yield. Similar to apples, pears are very cleansing and full of a range of vitamins, minerals and fibre. *Preparation: Wash well. For juicing, simply remove stalk and cut into pieces small enough to fit through your juicer. For smoothies, core and chop.*

**Pineapple** — The delicious flesh of the pineapple is a perfect juice or smoothie ingredient. It is rich in a range of vitamins and minerals, but is particularly known for an alkaline substance called bromelain, which aids digestion and is linked to a reduction of inflammation in arthritis and other inflammatory disorders. Choose a pineapple that is a deep, yellow colour and gives off a sweet scent from the bottom. *Preparation: Chop off the top and bottom of the fruit, and slice down the sides to remove the skin. If blending, remove any remaining eyes (there's no need if you are juicing).*

**Banana** — Completely unjuiceable, but a wonderful staple for blended drinks, turning a smoothie into a meal in itself. As with most fruit the riper the banana, the richer the flavour, and they're even good in a drink when they are past their eating best. A banana is a nutritional powerhouse – full of fibre, vitamins and minerals, as well as carbohydrates which are a key source of energy. *Preparation: Peel and break or slice into pieces.*

**Mango** — Mangoes, one of nature's most sumptuous fruits, come in a variety of colours and sizes, although my favourite are the amber Alfonse variety from India (usually available in late spring). Otherwise, choose your mango carefully to avoid disappointment: look out for one that yields slightly to the thumb and smells sweet (don't be fooled by the colour, as some green mangoes are perfectly ripe). Mangoes are extremely rich in beta-carotene, as well as minerals such as magnesium. *Preparation: Peel and slice flesh away from the stone. (Then chew and suck it unashamedly!)*

**Papaya** — One of the Tropics' wonderfoods, the papaya (or paw paw) is packed with beta-carotene, enzymes that help digestion, vitamin C and fibre. It comes in several varieties, although the most common is the more squat, pear-shaped type. Papayas are ripe when they are fully amber in colour and yield to gentle pressure. *Preparation: Peel, remove seeds, and slice into chunks.*

Drinks based on a variety of **berries** (including some recipes containing raspberries and strawberries) appear under this pictorial tab in the smoothie chapter.

> **Blackberry** — One of the few fruits that we can continue to pick wild. All the scratches are worth the effort for a pile of freshly picked, plump blackberries. Otherwise, nip down to the local green-grocer store. Blackberries are rich in antioxidants, particularly vitamin C. *Preparation: Wash well. Discard any berries that are mouldy or still attached to the hulls.*

**Blackcurrant** — Sharp but not sour, perfectly ripe blackcurrants add a strong flavour to any drink. They are an extremely rich source of vitamin C and other antioxidant nutrients. Crunch their seeds well in a blended drink as they contain healthy essential fats. *Preparation: Wash well. Remove any stalks and discard any berries that are mouldy.*

**Blueberry** — Small in size, big in flavour and goodness, blueberries are laden with antioxidant nutrients such as vitamins A and C, as well as bioflavonoids. They yield a rich, sweet flavour and give a blended drink blue specks. The berries are good for overcoming bladder problems, as well as boosting immunity and protecting the eyes and blood vessels. *Preparation: Wash well. Remove any stalks and discard any berries that are mouldy.*

**Cranberry** — Cranberries are excellent therapy for male and female urinary-tract problems but only in their pure, unsweetened form – the sweeteners often present in commercial drinks can aggravate such conditions. Because they are rather tart, cranberries are best mixed with other fruits. Like all berries, they are rich in a range of antioxidant nutrients. *Preparation: Wash well. Remove any stalks and discard any berries that are spoiled.*

Drinks using fruits belonging to the **melon** family are listed under this pictorial tab (they appear only in chapter three).

**Cantaloupe/Honeydew** — These are the most widely available varieties of melon. The orange-fleshed cantaloupe is particularly high in beta-carotene, but both kinds are rich in a range of vital nutrients, especially vitamin C. They have diuretic properties, meaning that they help eliminate excess fluid from the body. Choose melons that are firm, but yield slightly to pressing and that smell sweet. *Preparation: Halve, slice and cut the flesh away from the rind. Chop into chunks.*

**Watermelon** — Loaded with water and minerals, watermelon is one of the easiest healthfoods to digest.

Its redness indicates its high levels of beta-carotene, although it is also rich in minerals, especially potassium, and is a great cleanser. Blitz the seeds in the blender too, for extra zinc and vitamin E. Choose a watermelon that feels heavy for its size and makes a hollow sound when tapped. *Preparation: Cut out a wedge from the whole fruit and cut the flesh away from the rind. Chop to fit.*

**Strawberry** — Probably the most abundant and popular berry in the West, the strawberry is also one of the richest food sources of vitamin C. It is also abundant in a range of beneficial minerals, especially calcium which is good for bones and teeth. *Preparation: Wash well and, if blending, remove hulls (no need if juicing).*

The following fruits also appear in the recipes, but not as base ingredients. However, it is worth noting their nutritional value.

**Date** — Clearly not for juicing, but dates provide a rich, natural sweetness to a smoothie and load it with energy from the sugar. They're also a useful source of vitamin C. The best are the large, soft, sticky Medjool variety. *Preparation: Wash, halve and remove the pits.*

**Grape** — The grape is a very cleansing, alkaline, nutritious fruit, which is why grape-juice diets have been used for many years to heal chronic illnesses. The seedless varieties of either green or red grapes should be used for drinks, although red grapes are richer in antioxidants, notably those which can help reduce the threat of heart disease. *Preparation: Wash well.*

**Guava** — Not easy to get hold of, but if you do come across some guavas, they make fantastic, tropical additions to a drink. Choose fruits with a green-yellow skin – the fruit and the juice will be white to pink. Many stores sell guava nectar, but be sure to buy unsweetened brands. *Preparation: Peel, halve, remove seeds and chop into chunks.*

**Kiwi** — The brown, hairy exterior of the kiwi fruit belies its beautiful green interior with magically patterned black seeds. One of the richest sources of vitamin C, kiwis are also laden with beneficial minerals, especially potassium. Unfortunately, like much fresh produce these days, they are usually picked too early, but will ripen at home – just make sure they don't get too soft and develop a sweet acetone flavour. *Preparation: Peel and chop into chunks.*

**Lemon** — Too tart to ever be drunk neat, lemon juice is perfect for toning down the sweetness or saltiness of other juices, or even for being diluted with hot or cold water. Rich in vitamin C and bioflavonoids (mainly in the pith), lemons are also high in a range of minerals and are a particularly good source of potassium. To extract the maximum amount of juice, choose lemons that are heavy given their size and feel slightly soft. *Preparation: If juicing, peel and chop into chunks. If squeezing, cut in half.*

**Lime** — The smaller, green relative of lemons, limes have similar health properties and add a wonderful tropical tang to juices. *Preparation: If juicing, peel and chop into chunks. If squeezing, cut in half.*

**Passion fruit** — The uglier and wrinklier the passion fruit, the more likely it is to be full and juicy. Each fruit should have orange flesh, grey seeds and a pink inner lining. Passion fruit is a good source of vitamin C and has a richly perfumed flavour that stands out in almost any drink. *Preparation: Cut in half and scoop out flesh.*

**Tangerine** — Similar to the orange, but sweeter and with a far looser skin, any one of the tangerine/clementine family are a refreshing, milder alternative to this staple juice. Although you get the most juice by squeezing tangerines, putting them through a juicer will give you bioflavonoids in the pith. *Preparation: If juicing, peel and chop into chunks. If squeezing, cut in half.*

## vegetables

There are few vegetable juices, other than carrot, that are drinkable neat: most are simply not palatable enough. They are also generally too strong and should be diluted with other juices.

**Carrot** — The sweetest and best-tasting of vegetable juices, carrots are packed with vitamins and minerals, not least the antioxidant beta-carotene. The carrot's overall nutrient value makes it an immune-boosting, skin-clearing, digestion-supporting drink. *Preparation: Scrub well, top and tail and cut to fit.*

**Cucumber** — Cucumber juice is surprisingly flavourful, given the bland nature of the vegetable. Because of its mineral balance and high water content, cucumber is one of the best, natural diuretics known. Choose firm, dark cucumbers. *Preparation: Wash well and chop to fit.*

**Green vegetable** juice drinks are listed under this pictorial tab which can be found in chapter two.

> **Watercress** — Watercress is a very powerful cleanser owing to its high chlorophyll and sulphur contents. It is good for digestion, the skin, the circulation and the bladder, and is an exceptional, all-round juice. Because it is so potent, watercress is best well-diluted with other juices. Choose only green leaves, discarding any that have started to go yellow. *Preparation: Wash well.*
>
> **Broccoli** — With even more vitamin C than oranges (pound for pound), broccoli is loaded with important antioxidant and cleansing nutrients, some of which have been shown to protect against cancer. Choose compact, green heads for the freshest, most nutritious juice. *Preparation: Wash well and cut to fit your juicer.*
>
> **Cabbage** — Although on its own it is not particularly palatable as a juice, cabbage is worth slipping into other juices for its far-reaching health properties. Like other members of its family (broccoli, kale and so on), cabbage is

full of vitamins, minerals and anti-cancer nutrients. It is also soothing for stomach problems, including ulcers. *Preparation: Remove outer leaves and cut off pieces to fit.*

**Kale** — One of nature's wonderfoods, kale is loaded with vitamins (especially A and C) and minerals as well as anti-cancer nutrients. As such it is a very cleansing, immune-boosting, skin-healing, bone-building, generally excellent all-round health bonanza. *Preparation: Wash well.*

**Lettuce** — Choose the darker varieties, which tend to be richer in all minerals and vitamins. Lettuce is cleansing because of the combination of nutrients and high water content, but it is also known for its sedative properties and is best added to juices as a relaxant or sleep aid. *Preparation: Wash leaves well.*

**Parsley** — Parsley is one of the top ingredients in the health stakes. Its dark green colour comes from its rich chlorophyll content, which makes it highly cleansing. Parsley is also good for aiding digestion and for generally providing the body with a stack of minerals and vitamins. *Preparation: Wash well.*

**Spinach** — Exceptionally rich in vitamin C, beta-carotene and iron, spinach is also highly cleansing and is laden with health-boosting, regenerative properties. These tone the digestive system, the liver and the circulation. However, it is high in oxalic acid, which interferes with calcium absorption, so spinach juice should not be drunk in large quantities. Choose small, bright green leaves. *Preparation: Wash well.*

**Root vegetable** juice drinks (other than the carrot) can be found under this pictorial tab in chapter two.

**Beet (beetroot)** — The wonderful juice of beet has a distinctly "soily" taste to it. This earthiness gives a hint of the very rich mineral and vitamin content, and as such, beet is one of the most cleansing, blood-boosting, tonic-like juices there is. Juice the greens too, if you can get hold of them, as they add an even greater health dimension. *Preparation: Top and tail, scrub well and cut to fit.*

**Parsnip** — This white relative of the carrot provides a sweet, earthy touch to a juice, as well as an all-round dose of minerals and vitamins for the body. Parsnip is rich in the trace elements sulphur and silicon, good for healthy hair, skin and nails. *Preparation: Scrub well, top and tail and cut to fit.*

**Sweet potato** — Not related to the potato, sweet potatoes are generally easier to digest and higher in fibre than their namesakes. They are also a rich source of beta-carotene. Sweet potatoes are soothing to the digestive tract, cleansing, and have an alkalizing effect on the body. *Preparation: Scrub well and cut to fit.*

**Tomato** — Although strictly speaking a fruit, the tomato is commonly classed as a vegetable as it has a savoury rather than a sweet taste. Tomatoes taste quite acidic, but, in fact, have a soothing effect on the body. They offer nutrients which can ease problems with digestion, the liver and the skin. Tomatoes also contain lycopene, an antioxidant shown to help prostate problems. *Preparation: Wash well and slice to fit.*

**Celery** — A refreshing, salty juice, celery complements other vegetable juice flavours by cutting through some of the richer, sweeter tastes. Celery is a very cleansing, soothing juice, with diuretic properties (helping to rid the body of excess water). Choose greener stems, not those that are wilting or bendy. Juice the whole stick, including the leaves. *Preparation: Scrub well.*

**Other ingredients** used in some of the recipes in this book include the following:

> **Bell Peppers** — Also called peppers or capsicum, red, green and yellow bell peppers add a sweet flavour to juice and are an excellent source of antioxidants, particularly vitamin C and beta-carotene. *Preparation: Wash well and slice.*
>
> **Ginger** — An age-old natural remedy, the root of the ginger plant helps improve digestion and circulation, and relieves nausea, bloating, colds, sore throats and inflammation of any sort. *Preparation: Wash well, peel if shrivelled and slice.*
>
> **Mint** — This aromatic herb is a refreshing, soothing addition to a drink. It helps to enhance digestion and calm the digestive tract, quell nausea and relieve cramps. The menthol in mint can also soothe congestion in the respiratory tract. Choose fresh, deep green leaves. *Preparation: Wash well.*

## healthy additives

You can enhance the health properties of your juice or smoothie even further by adding certain vitamin and mineral supplements, and other health-enhancing foods. Some of the additives are best blended with smoothies only, as they don't mix well in a pure, liquid juice.

### additives for juices or smoothies

**Vitamin and mineral drops/powder** — Some companies make excellent vitamins and minerals in the form of liquid drops or powders. Adding them to your daily juice or smoothie is a good way of taking them, especially for children.

**Herbal drops** — If you take herbal medicines, such as echinacea or a blend from your herbalist, mixing them with a juice may be a more palatable option. (Check with your herbalist whether or not mixing with just water may be better.)

**Spirulina/Barleygrass/Wheatgrass powder** — Dense forms of nutrients especially rich in cleansing chlorophyll, these three are nature's wonderfoods in a green powder. If you're mixing one with juice, best to shake it with a little juice in a jar before blending it with the rest.

## smoothie-only additives

**Wheatgerm** — Most of the goodness in a grain of wheat is found in the germ – a great additive to smoothies for an extra boost of vitamins and minerals, particularly vitamins B and E.

**Flaxseeds** — Also known as linseeds, one of the richest vegetarian sources of essential fatty acids, as well as vitamins and minerals.

**Pumpkin/sunflower seeds** — These not only give smoothies a nutty, crunchy taste and texture, but also increase their vitamin, mineral and essential fatty acid content.

**Cold-pressed seed oils** — Far from the usual commercial varieties, cold-pressed oils, such as from sunflower or pumpkin seeds, offer unadulterated sources of essential fatty acids.

**Tahini** — This creamed sesame seed paste adds a distinctive flavour to any smoothie, as well as boosting its nutrient content.

**Blackstrap molasses** — Derived from the whole cane from which sugar is extracted, syrupy sweet molasses is laden with minerals (particularly iron and calcium) and B-vitamins.

**Lecithin** — Part of every cell of the body, lecithin is particularly important for the digestion of fats and for healthy nerve and brain cells. Add it to your smoothie in powder form.

**Brewer's yeast** — This is one of the best sources of B-vitamins available, and also contains a host of vital minerals.

# making
# juices
## chapter 2

Once you start on the adventure of making a fresh juice
every day, you will be hooked. By now you are aware of
the delights and benefits of pressing your own juice and
here's where the actual process begins. You've got the
juicer (you may even have used it), what follows on the
next pages are 220 blends to stimulate both your palate
and your imagination.

We begin with juices based on fruits (blends 1–128),
followed by juices based on vegetables (blends 129–220).
Each recipe makes two portions unless otherwise stated.
If you feel you'd like some guidance on which recipes to
try first, you may like to experiment with The Basic Intro
Week (see p.176) which will gently introduce you to the
idea of blending different fruits and a few vegetables.
Guidelines for preparing the ingredients are given on
pages 14 to 24, so simply get them ready and juice away!

# top tips

Below are a few reminders, and helpful hints, tips and suggestions to enable you to get the most from your juicing.

1   When selecting fruit to juice, choose pieces that are almost but not quite ripe, as these tend to yield the maximum amount of juice and the best taste from your juicer.

2   Avoid juicing fruits that are over-ripe or too soft as these generally do not pass well through a juicer.

3   Get into the habit of always washing your juicer immediately after use, when it is much easier to clean.

4   To get the most out of citrus fruits, extract the juice using a citrus press rather than a juicer.

5   While all fruit and veg must be washed well before use, avoid soaking them as this can weaken their nutrient content.

6   If you do peel your fruit or veg, do it as finely as possible so as to preserve as many of the vital nutrients as you can.

7   To prevent juices from going even slightly brown (that is oxidizing and damaging their nutrient content), drink them immediately or pour them into a jug containing a squeeze of lemon juice or a spoon of vitamin C powder.

8   Dilute your vegetable juices with a little water if you find them too strong-tasting. Always dilute vegetable juices for children.

9   If you find that your energy levels fluctuate throughout the day, emphasize vegetable juices, and dilute any fruit juices you do have with water. Fruit juices contain high levels of natural sugar which give an immediate energy boost but can be followed by a dip in your energy level.

10   Although you won't ever be stuck for recipes using this book, be experimental and create your own blends using whatever you have in the refrigerator and fruit bowl.

# 001 | eve's downfall

4 apples

I always have a sense that if you're going to make the effort to make a juice then make it interesting, but pure, freshly pressed apple juice is exquisite and you can't beat the home-made frothy, delicate green version. My favourite are Granny Smith or Egremont Russets but you could juice any type of apple you like.

**NUTRIENTS**

Beta-carotene, folic acid, vitamin C; calcium, magnesium, phosphorus, potassium, sulphur

ENERGY ★★★★★
DETOX ★★★★☆
IMMUNITY ★★☆☆☆
DIGESTION ★★★☆☆
SKIN ★★★☆☆

# 002 | apple basic

3 apples
2 carrots

Most of us can rustle up a few apples from the fruit bowl and carrots from the refrigerator. This delicious but simple combination is a good way to introduce carrot to your juice repertoire if you're not used to vegetable juices.

**NUTRIENTS**

Beta-carotene, folic acid, vitamin C; calcium, magnesium, phosphorus, potassium, sodium, sulphur

ENERGY ★★★★☆
DETOX ★★★★☆
IMMUNITY ★★☆☆☆
DIGESTION ★★☆☆☆
SKIN ★★★★☆

# 003 | ocean deep

4 apples
1 teaspoon spirulina

The combination of the pale green apple juice and dark green spirulina powder makes this power-packed juice look like the deep, green sea. Shake the spirulina with a little of the juice in a jar before mixing it with the rest.

**NUTRIENTS**

Beta-carotene, folic acid, vitamins B1, B2, B3, B5, B6 and C; calcium, magnesium, phosphorus, potassium, sulphur; protein, essential fatty acids

ENERGY ★★★★☆
DETOX ★★★★☆
IMMUNITY ★★★☆☆
DIGESTION ★★☆☆☆
SKIN ★★★★☆

## 004 | basic with a boost

3 apples
2 carrots
½ inch (1 cm) ginger root
1 teaspoon spirulina

The addition of spirulina sends the nutritious value of this juice onto another plane. Stir or shake in the spirulina powder after you have made the juice.

**NUTRIENTS**

| | | |
|---|---|---|
| Beta-carotene, folic acid, vitamin C; | ENERGY | ★★★☆☆ |
| calcium, magnesium, phosphorus, | DETOX | ★★★★☆ |
| potassium, sulphur; protein, | IMMUNITY | ★★★☆☆ |
| essential fatty acids | DIGESTION | ★★★☆☆ |
| | SKIN | ★★★☆☆ |

## 005 | orchard blend

3 apples
1 pear

Made with classic orchard fruits, this sweet juice really makes you realize why apples and pears are the staples of a fruit bowl and not so boring after all.

**NUTRIENTS**

| | | |
|---|---|---|
| Beta-carotene, folic acid, vitamin C; | ENERGY | ★★★★☆ |
| calcium, magnesium, phosphorus, | DETOX | ★★☆☆☆ |
| potassium, sulphur | IMMUNITY | ★★☆☆☆ |
| | DIGESTION | ★★★☆☆ |
| | SKIN | ★★★☆☆ |

## 006 | apple blush

3 apples
1 nectarine
8 strawberries

The delicate colour of this juice gives only the slightest indication of the sensational taste, especially if you use a tangy variety of apple such as Granny Smith combined with sweet, ripe strawberries and nectarines.

**NUTRIENTS**

| | | |
|---|---|---|
| Beta-carotene, biotin, folic acid, | ENERGY | ★★★★★ |
| vitamin C; calcium, magnesium, | DETOX | ★★☆☆☆ |
| phosphorus, potassium, sulphur | IMMUNITY | ★★★☆☆ |
| | DIGESTION | ★☆☆☆☆ |
| | SKIN | ★★★★☆ |

## 007 | sweet 'n' savoury

3 apples
2 sticks celery

The saltiness of the celery nicely offsets the sweetness of the apples in this refreshing juice. It's a perfect thirst-quencher, especially if you use a sharp apple variety such as Granny Smith.

**NUTRIENTS**

Beta-carotene, folic acid, vitamin C;
calcium, magnesium, manganese,
phosphorus, potassium, sodium,
sulphur

| | |
|---|---|
| ENERGY | ★★☆☆☆ |
| DETOX | ★★★☆☆ |
| IMMUNITY | ★☆☆☆☆ |
| DIGESTION | ★★★☆☆ |
| SKIN | ★★★☆☆ |

## 008 | sweet c

3 apples
2 guavas

This is one of the few recipes for which I suggest using a sweeter variety of apple, such as Cox, to offset the tangy guava, which is a phenomenally rich source of vitamin C.

**NUTRIENTS**

Beta-carotene, folic acid, vitamin B3,
vitamin C; calcium, magnesium,
phosphorus, potassium, sodium,
sulphur

| | |
|---|---|
| ENERGY | ★★★★☆ |
| DETOX | ★★★☆☆ |
| IMMUNITY | ★★★★★ |
| DIGESTION | ★☆☆☆☆ |
| SKIN | ★★★★☆ |

## 009 | sweet c too

2 apples
2 oranges

You may think that oranges would completely overwhelm the delicate juice of the apples, but actually they really enhance it and make this drink a simple, refreshing start to the day. Remember that oranges are best juiced on a citrus press and added to the apple juice made in the extractor, although you can push peeled orange pieces through the juicer.

**NUTRIENTS**

Beta-carotene, folic acid, vitamin C;
calcium, magnesium, phosphorus,
potassium, sodium, sulphur

| | |
|---|---|
| ENERGY | ★★★★☆ |
| DETOX | ★★★☆☆ |
| IMMUNITY | ★★★★☆ |
| DIGESTION | ★☆☆☆☆ |
| SKIN | ★★★☆☆ |

## 010 | apple tropics

3 apples
$\frac{1}{2}$ pineapple
$\frac{1}{2}$ lime
$\frac{1}{2}$ passion fruit

An extra tang and taste of the tropics is evident in this apple recipe. It's best to stir the passion fruit into the juice once it's made, rather than passing it through the blender.

**NUTRIENTS**

Beta-carotene, folic acid, vitamin C; calcium, magnesium, manganese, phosphorus, potassium, sulphur

ENERGY      ★★★★☆
DETOX       ★★☆☆☆
IMMUNITY    ★★★☆☆
DIGESTION   ★★★★☆
SKIN        ★★★☆☆

## 011 | citrus apples

3 apples
2 tangerines
$\frac{1}{2}$ lime

The more delicate flavour of tangerines (or clementines or other such fruits, rather than oranges) adds a subtle layer around the apple, while the lime gives it a great afterbite.

**NUTRIENTS**

Beta-carotene, folic acid, vitamin C; calcium, magnesium, phosphorus, potassium, sodium, sulphur

ENERGY      ★★★☆☆
DETOX       ★★☆☆☆
IMMUNITY    ★★★★☆
DIGESTION   ★☆☆☆☆
SKIN        ★★★☆☆

# 012 | apple cleanser

2 apples
2 kale leaves
1 stick celery
$\frac{1}{3}$ long cucumber
$\frac{1}{2}$ beet (beetroot)

The fruitiness of the apples offsets the more challenging taste of the greens to produce this beautifully red detoxifying juice.

**NUTRIENTS**
Beta-carotene, folic acid, vitamin B3, vitamin C; calcium, iron, magnesium, manganese, phosphorus, potassium, sulphur

| | |
|---|---|
| ENERGY | ★★☆☆☆ |
| DETOX | ★★★★☆ |
| IMMUNITY | ★★★☆☆ |
| DIGESTION | ★★☆☆☆ |
| SKIN | ★★★☆☆ |

# 013 | winter crumble

2 apples
2 handfuls blackberries

I can't help but think of a hot pie or crumble when I make this juice. You could actually heat it up (but don't let it boil) after you've made it, for a warm drink on a cold night, but personally I like my juices cold.

**NUTRIENTS**
Beta-carotene, folic acid, vitamin B3, vitamin C; calcium, iron, magnesium, manganese, phosphorus, potassium, sodium, sulphur

| | |
|---|---|
| ENERGY | ★★★★★ |
| DETOX | ★★☆☆☆ |
| IMMUNITY | ★★★★☆ |
| DIGESTION | ★☆☆☆☆ |
| SKIN | ★★★★☆ |

## 014 | apple pie

4 apples
$\frac{1}{2}$ teaspoon ground cinnamon

It's quite hard to stir in the cinnamon powder – instead I suggest putting the juice in a jar and shaking it up to add the spicy kick.

**NUTRIENTS**

| Beta-carotene, folic acid, vitamin B3, | | ENERGY | ★★★★☆ |
|---|---|---|---|
| vitamin C; calcium, magnesium, | | DETOX | ★★★☆☆ |
| phosphorus, potassium, sodium, | | IMMUNITY | ★★☆☆☆ |
| sulphur | | DIGESTION | ★★★☆☆ |
| | | SKIN | ★★★☆☆ |

## 015 | apple blues

3 apples
2 good handfuls blueberries

If your blueberries are particularly sweet, choose a crisp, tangy apple such as Granny Smith; otherwise, use a sweeter type like Jonagold or Empire.

**NUTRIENTS**

| Beta-carotene, biotin, folic acid, | | ENERGY | ★★★★★ |
|---|---|---|---|
| vitamins B1, B2, B6, C and E; calcium, | | DETOX | ★★★☆☆ |
| chromium, magnesium, sodium | | IMMUNITY | ★★★★☆ |
| | | DIGESTION | ★☆☆☆☆ |
| | | SKIN | ★★★★☆ |

## 016 | black orchard berry buster

3 apples
2 good handfuls dark berries such as blueberries,
 blackcurrants or blackberries

It may seem a waste to juice plump, sweet berries, but I can't resist it sometimes. In the winter you can throw a few canned berries into the juicer but it's not quite the same thing.

**NUTRIENTS**

| Beta-carotene, folic acid, | | ENERGY | ★★★★★ |
|---|---|---|---|
| vitamins B1, B2, B6, C and E; calcium, | | DETOX | ★★★☆☆ |
| chromium, magnesium, manganese, | | IMMUNITY | ★★★★☆ |
| phosphorus, potassium, sodium, | | DIGESTION | ★☆☆☆☆ |
| sulphur | | SKIN | ★★★★☆ |

# 017 | pink orchard berry buster

3 apples
2 good handfuls red berries such as raspberries or
   strawberries

Another treat, using fresh, sweet berries in the summer to turn tangy
apple juice into a pastel thirst-quencher.

**NUTRIENTS**

| | | |
|---|---|---|
| Beta-carotene, biotin, folic acid, | ENERGY | ★★★☆☆ |
| vitamin C; calcium, magnesium, | DETOX | ★☆☆☆☆ |
| manganese, phosphorus, potassium, | IMMUNITY | ★★★★☆ |
| sodium, sulphur | DIGESTION | ★☆☆☆☆ |
| | SKIN | ★★★★☆ |

# 018 | double apple

2 apples
$\frac{1}{3}$ pineapple
1 small bunch fresh mint

Living in Bangkok, apples were a luxury, unlike the ubiquitous pineapple.
Unfortunately, it's completely the other way around in most other parts of
the world. Use sweeter apples such as Cox to match with the amazing juicy
tang of the pineapple, which is particularly helpful for digestion.

**NUTRIENTS**

| | | |
|---|---|---|
| Beta-carotene, folic acid, vitamin B3, | ENERGY | ★★★☆☆ |
| vitamin C; calcium, magnesium, | DETOX | ★☆☆☆☆ |
| manganese, phosphorus, potassium, | IMMUNITY | ★★★☆☆ |
| sodium, sulphur | DIGESTION | ★★★★★ |
| | SKIN | ★★☆☆☆ |

# 019 | waldorf salad

2 apples
2 sticks celery
1 tablespoon (15 ml) cold-pressed hemp-seed oil

This one reminds me of a Waldorf salad, without the walnuts but with the
hemp-seed oil to give you a similar benefit of omega 3 fatty acids. The oil will
blend best if it's shaken with the juice in a jar.

**NUTRIENTS**

| | | |
|---|---|---|
| Beta-carotene, folic acid, vitamin C; | ENERGY | ★★★★☆ |
| calcium, magnesium, manganese, | DETOX | ★★★☆☆ |
| phosphorus, potassium, sodium, | IMMUNITY | ★★★☆☆ |
| sulphur; essential fatty acids | DIGESTION | ★★★☆☆ |
| | SKIN | ★★★☆☆ |

## 020 | bleeding apples

3 apples
$\frac{1}{2}$ beet (beetroot)

The colour of beet overtakes any other juice and gives it a deep,
earthy flavour. This recipe is a gentle introduction to the powerful
juice of this root vegetable. For heftier doses, see pp.95–6.

**NUTRIENTS**

Beta-carotene, folic acid, vitamin C;
calcium, magnesium, phosphorus,
potassium, sodium, sulphur

| | |
|---|---|
| ENERGY | ★★★★☆ |
| DETOX | ★★★★★ |
| IMMUNITY | ★★☆☆☆ |
| DIGESTION | ★★☆☆☆ |
| SKIN | ★★★☆☆ |

## 021 | apple tang

3 apples
1 grapefruit
1 lime

The sweetness of the apple – best to use a sweet variety – combines
well with the grapefruit and lime.

**NUTRIENTS**

Beta-carotene, folic acid, vitamin C;
calcium, magnesium, phosphorus,
potassium, sodium, sulphur

| | |
|---|---|
| ENERGY | ★★★★☆ |
| DETOX | ★★☆☆☆ |
| IMMUNITY | ★★★☆☆ |
| DIGESTION | ★☆☆☆☆ |
| SKIN | ★★★☆☆ |

## 022 | apple gone loupey

3 apples
2 thick slices of melon
1 small bunch fresh mint

To contrast with the sweetness of a ripe melon, it's best to use a sharper
apple variety such as Egremont Russet or Granny Smith.

**NUTRIENTS**

Beta-carotene, folic acid, vitamin C;
calcium, magnesium, phosphorus,
potassium, sodium, sulphur

| | |
|---|---|
| ENERGY | ★★★★★ |
| DETOX | ★★★☆☆ |
| IMMUNITY | ★★★☆☆ |
| DIGESTION | ★☆☆☆☆ |
| SKIN | ★★★★☆ |

## 023 | waterapple

3 apples
2 thick slices of watermelon
1 lime

I would usually use watermelon to make a fresh smoothie (see p.136), but this juice combination is irresistible. Use a sharp type of apple.

**NUTRIENTS**

| | | |
|---|---|---|
| Beta-carotene, folic acid, vitamin C; | ENERGY | ★★★★★ |
| calcium, magnesium, phosphorus, | DETOX | ★★★★☆ |
| potassium, sulphur | IMMUNITY | ★★★☆☆ |
| | DIGESTION | ★☆☆☆☆ |
| | SKIN | ★★★★☆ |

## 024 | apple lullaby

2 apples
$\frac{1}{4}$ lettuce
$\frac{1}{2}$ lemon
(makes one glass of juice)

The lettuce is the key sleep-inducing ingredient in this juice. Best drunk just as you plan to hit the pillow. You can use any variety of lettuce.

**NUTRIENTS**

| | | |
|---|---|---|
| Beta-carotene, folic acid, vitamin C; | ENERGY | ★☆☆☆☆ |
| calcium, magnesium, phosphorus, | DETOX | ★★★☆☆ |
| potassium, sulphur | IMMUNITY | ★★★☆☆ |
| | DIGESTION | ★☆☆☆☆ |
| | SKIN | ★★★☆☆ |

## 025 | grape ape

3 apples
1 bunch red grapes
1 nectarine

Very cleansing and refreshing, choose a variety of apple that contrasts with the level of sweetness of the grapes, and use a nectarine (or peach) that is ripe enough to yield to a gentle press of your thumb.

**NUTRIENTS**

| | | |
|---|---|---|
| Beta-carotene, folic acid, vitamin C, | ENERGY | ★★★★★ |
| vitamin E; calcium, magnesium, | DETOX | ★★★☆☆ |
| manganese, phosphorus, | IMMUNITY | ★★★☆☆ |
| potassium, sulphur | DIGESTION | ★☆☆☆☆ |
| | SKIN | ★★★★☆ |

## 026 | parsnapple

3 apples
2 parsnips
sprinkling of grated nutmeg

I certainly turned my nose up when I first heard of the concept of
juicing a parsnip, but actually, it's deliciously sweet. Blend it with a
sharp apple variety. You can leave out the nutmeg if you don't feel
like shaking it all up, otherwise it'll just sit on top.

**NUTRIENTS**

Beta-carotene, folic acid, vitamin C;
calcium, magnesium, phosphorus,
potassium, sodium, sulphur

| | |
|---|---|
| ENERGY | ★★★☆☆ |
| DETOX | ★★★☆☆ |
| IMMUNITY | ★★☆☆☆ |
| DIGESTION | ★☆☆☆☆ |
| SKIN | ★★★☆☆ |

## 027 | apple zing

3 apples
2 carrots
$\frac{1}{2}$ inch (1 cm) ginger root

Basic with a bite – the ginger gives a sharp snap to an otherwise
sweet juice. Just snap or slice off a piece of ginger root and juice
it with the other ingredients

**NUTRIENTS**

Beta-carotene, folic acid, vitamin C;
calcium, magnesium, phosphorus,
potassium, sulphur

| | |
|---|---|
| ENERGY | ★★★★☆ |
| DETOX | ★★★☆☆ |
| IMMUNITY | ★★★☆☆ |
| DIGESTION | ★★★★☆ |
| SKIN | ★★★★☆ |

# 028 | cranapple

3 apples
1 handful cranberries
1 handful grapes

Although cranberries are best known for combating urinary tract infections, they are also delicious, tangy and great for the immune system in general. Use sweet varieties of apples and grapes to offset the sharpness of the cranberries.

**NUTRIENTS**

Beta-carotene, folic acid, vitamin C, vitamin E; calcium, iron, magnesium, manganese, phosphorus, potassium, sulphur

| | |
|---|---|
| ENERGY | ★★★★★ |
| DETOX | ★★☆☆☆ |
| IMMUNITY | ★★★★☆ |
| DIGESTION | ★★☆☆☆ |
| SKIN | ★★★★☆ |

# 029 | prime cooler

3 apples
½ long cucumber
1 inch (2.5 cm) ginger root
1 small bunch fresh mint

There are few juice blends which are quite so refreshing – the sweetness of the apple is offset by the watery cucumber and sharpened by the ginger and mint.

**NUTRIENTS**

Beta-carotene, folic acid, vitamin C; calcium, magnesium, phosphorus, potassium, sodium, sulphur

| | |
|---|---|
| ENERGY | ★★☆☆☆ |
| DETOX | ★★★☆☆ |
| IMMUNITY | ★★☆☆☆ |
| DIGESTION | ★★★☆☆ |
| SKIN | ★★★☆☆ |

# 030 | bellyful

3 apples
¼ white cabbage
¼ small fennel bulb
1 small bunch fresh mint

This combination is an excellent one for soothing the digestive system. The cabbage is especially good for the stomach.

**NUTRIENTS**

Beta-carotene, folic acid, vitamin C, vitamin E; calcium, magnesium, phosphorus, potassium, sodium, sulphur

| | |
|---|---|
| ENERGY | ★★☆☆☆ |
| DETOX | ★★★☆☆ |
| IMMUNITY | ★★☆☆☆ |
| DIGESTION | ★★★★★ |
| SKIN | ★★★☆☆ |

## 031 | pure grapefruit

3 grapefruits

Another firm favourite all on its own, whether you prefer it made
with sharper white fruit or the sweeter pink or ruby varieties.

**NUTRIENTS**

Beta-carotene, folic acid, vitamin C;
calcium, magnesium, phosphorus,
potassium, sulphur

| | |
|---|---|
| ENERGY | ★★★★★ |
| DETOX | ★☆☆☆☆ |
| IMMUNITY | ★★★★☆ |
| DIGESTION | ☆☆☆☆☆ |
| SKIN | ★★☆☆☆ |

## 032 | grapefruit sharp

2 grapefruits
1 lemon
1 lime

You really will want to use sweet pink grapefruits for this one,
unless you enjoy that eye-watering sourness.

**NUTRIENTS**

Beta-carotene, folic acid, vitamin C;
calcium, magnesium, phosphorus,
potassium, sodium, sulphur

| | |
|---|---|
| ENERGY | ★★★★☆ |
| DETOX | ★☆☆☆☆ |
| IMMUNITY | ★★★★★ |
| DIGESTION | ★☆☆☆☆ |
| SKIN | ★★☆☆☆ |

## 033 | grapefruit sweet

2 grapefruits
2 tangerines

I prefer using white grapefruits for this one to contrast with the
sweetness of tangerines or clementines.

**NUTRIENTS**

Beta-carotene, folic acid, vitamin C;
calcium, magnesium, phosphorus,
potassium, sodium, sulphur

| | |
|---|---|
| ENERGY | ★★★★☆ |
| DETOX | ★☆☆☆☆ |
| IMMUNITY | ★★★★☆ |
| DIGESTION | ★☆☆☆☆ |
| SKIN | ★★☆☆☆ |

# 034 | grapefruit basic

1 grapefruit
1 apple
2 carrots
1 stick celery

Another one of my stock blends for a good wake-up call in the morning.

**NUTRIENTS**

Beta-carotene, folic acid, vitamin C;
calcium, magnesium, manganese,
phosphorus, potassium, sodium,
sulphur

| | |
|---|---|
| ENERGY | ★★★★☆ |
| DETOX | ★★★☆☆ |
| IMMUNITY | ★★★★☆ |
| DIGESTION | ★☆☆☆☆ |
| SKIN | ★★★☆☆ |

# 035 | grapefruit basic with a bite

1 grapefruit
1 apple
2 carrots
1 stick celery
$\frac{1}{2}$ inch (1 cm) ginger root

This is the Basic with a sharp kick from the ginger, particularly good
if you've got a cold.

**NUTRIENTS**

Beta-carotene, folic acid, vitamin C;
calcium, magnesium, manganese,
phosphorus, potassium, sodium,
sulphur

| | |
|---|---|
| ENERGY | ★★★★☆ |
| DETOX | ★★★☆☆ |
| IMMUNITY | ★★★☆☆ |
| DIGESTION | ★★☆☆☆ |
| SKIN | ★★★☆☆ |

# 036 | water cooler

2 grapefruits
1 thick slice watermelon

I have a slight preference for this over Water Cooler II (see p.54) because the
contrast of flavours and textures is even better.

**NUTRIENTS**

Beta-carotene, folic acid, vitamin C;
calcium, iron, magnesium, phosphorus,
potassium, sodium, sulphur

| | |
|---|---|
| ENERGY | ★★★★☆ |
| DETOX | ★★☆☆☆ |
| IMMUNITY | ★★★★☆ |
| DIGESTION | ☆☆☆☆☆ |
| SKIN | ★★★☆☆ |

## 037 | grapefruit blues

2 grapefruits
1 large handful blueberries

Whether you choose a tangy white grapefruit or sweeter pink variety,
the addition of the blueberries will transform the colour and give an
extra antioxidant lift.

### NUTRIENTS

Beta-carotene, biotin, folic acid,
vitamins B1, B2, B6, C and E; calcium,
chromium, magnesium, phosphorus,
potassium, sodium, sulphur

| | |
|---|---|
| ENERGY | ★★★★☆ |
| DETOX | ★★☆☆☆ |
| IMMUNITY | ★★★★★ |
| DIGESTION | ☆☆☆☆☆ |
| SKIN | ★★★★☆ |

## 038 | pink grapefruit

2 grapefruits
1 handful raspberries
1 handful strawberries

Just the colour of this makes you want to schlurp it up, not to mention
how great it is for your body's defences.

### NUTRIENTS

Beta-carotene, biotin, folic acid,
vitamin C; calcium, magnesium,
manganese, phosphorus, potassium,
sodium, sulphur

| | |
|---|---|
| ENERGY | ★★★★☆ |
| DETOX | ★☆☆☆☆ |
| IMMUNITY | ★★★★★ |
| DIGESTION | ☆☆☆☆☆ |
| SKIN | ★★★★☆ |

## 039 | greatfruit c

2 grapefruits
1 guava
1 kiwi

Not just for colds, high doses of vitamin C such as are found in this tasty
drink can ward off all sorts of other illnesses and aging.

### NUTRIENTS

Beta-carotene, folic acid, vitamin C;
calcium, magnesium, phosphorus,
potassium, sodium, sulphur

| | |
|---|---|
| ENERGY | ★★★★☆ |
| DETOX | ★★★☆☆ |
| IMMUNITY | ★★★★★ |
| DIGESTION | ☆☆☆☆☆ |
| SKIN | ★★★★☆ |

# 040 | surprising sweetie

2 grapefruits
1 thick slice of melon
1 peach

You would never imagine that anything with grapefruit could be so
sweet, let alone pack such an immune-boosting punch.

### NUTRIENTS

Beta-carotene, folic acid, vitamin B3,
vitamin C; calcium, magnesium,
phosphorus, potassium, sodium,
sulphur

| | |
|---|---|
| ENERGY | ★★★★☆ |
| DETOX | ★★☆☆☆ |
| IMMUNITY | ★★★★☆ |
| DIGESTION | ★★☆☆☆ |
| SKIN | ★★★★★ |

# 041 | pale faced

2 grapefruits
1 apple
$\frac{1}{2}$ bulb fennel
1 small bunch fresh mint

A blend of three distinctly strong flavours makes a delicious whole,
with the more subtle undertones of the apple.

### NUTRIENTS

Beta-carotene, folic acid, vitamin C;
calcium, magnesium, phosphorus,
potassium, sodium, sulphur

| | |
|---|---|
| ENERGY | ★★★★☆ |
| DETOX | ★☆☆☆☆ |
| IMMUNITY | ★★☆☆☆ |
| DIGESTION | ★★★☆☆ |
| SKIN | ★★☆☆☆ |

# 042 | grapefruit tonic

3 grapefruits
1 teaspoon spirulina

Simple but strong, the earthy taste of spirulina goes well with grapefruit.
Best shaken in a jar with the juice to avoid lumps of spirulina powder.

### NUTRIENTS

Beta-carotene, folic acid, vitamins B1, B3,
B5, B6 and C; calcium, iron, magnesium,
phosphorus, potassium, sodium, sulphur;
protein; essential fatty acids

| | |
|---|---|
| ENERGY | ★★★★☆ |
| DETOX | ★★★★☆ |
| IMMUNITY | ★★★☆☆ |
| DIGESTION | ★☆☆☆☆ |
| SKIN | ★★★★☆ |

## 043 | peppery grapefruit

2 grapefruits
$\frac{1}{4}$ red cabbage

It's the strong red cabbage here which gives this juice its distinctive,
peppery taste and vibrant colour.

**NUTRIENTS**

Beta-carotene, folic acid, vitamin C,
vitamin E; calcium, magnesium,
phosphorus, potassium, sodium, sulphur

| | |
|---|---|
| ENERGY | ★★★☆☆ |
| DETOX | ★☆☆☆☆ |
| IMMUNITY | ★★★★☆ |
| DIGESTION | ★★★☆☆ |
| SKIN | ★★☆☆☆ |

## 044 | orange morning

2 grapefruits
3 carrots
$\frac{1}{2}$ inch (1 cm) ginger root

Another great morning staple but one where the sharp, awakening
grapefruit tang is tempered by the sweet, rich carrot.

**NUTRIENTS**

Beta-carotene, folic acid, vitamin C;
calcium, magnesium, phosphorus,
potassium, sodium, sulphur

| | |
|---|---|
| ENERGY | ★★★★☆ |
| DETOX | ★★★☆☆ |
| IMMUNITY | ★★★★☆ |
| DIGESTION | ★★★☆☆ |
| SKIN | ★★★☆☆ |

## 045 | grapefruit greens

2 grapefruits
1 handful watercress
1 bunch parsley

You can certainly taste the cleansing goodness in this one, and the
strong flavour of the grapefruit can carry the greens' taste very well.

**NUTRIENTS**

Beta-carotene, folic acid, vitamins B3,
C and E; calcium, iron, magnesium,
phosphorus, potassium, sodium, sulphur

| | |
|---|---|
| ENERGY | ★★★☆☆ |
| DETOX | ★★★☆☆ |
| IMMUNITY | ★★☆☆☆ |
| DIGESTION | ★☆☆☆☆ |
| SKIN | ★★★☆☆ |

# 046 | black grapefruit

2 grapefruits
1 handful blackberries
1 handful blackcurrants

A fabulous contrast of the colours as they blend in the jug… and then a
fantastic boost to immunity. Best made in summer with fresh berries.

**NUTRIENTS**

Beta-carotene, folic acid, vitamins B5,
C and E; calcium, iron, magnesium,
manganese, phosphorus, potassium,
sodium, sulphur

| | |
|---|---|
| ENERGY | ★★★★☆ |
| DETOX | ★☆☆☆☆ |
| IMMUNITY | ★★★★★ |
| DIGESTION | ☆☆☆☆☆ |
| SKIN | ★★★★☆ |

# 047 | cloudy day

2 grapefruits
$\frac{1}{2}$ long cucumber
2 sticks celery
1 small bunch fresh mint

The sweet tang of the grapefruit contrasts wonderfully with the almost
melon-like cucumber and salty celery, all lifted by the mint.

**NUTRIENTS**

Beta-carotene, folic acid, vitamin C;
calcium, magnesium, phosphorus,
potassium, sodium, sulphur

| | |
|---|---|
| ENERGY | ★★★☆☆ |
| DETOX | ★★☆☆☆ |
| IMMUNITY | ★★☆☆☆ |
| DIGESTION | ★★☆☆☆ |
| SKIN | ★★☆☆☆ |

## 048 | bleeding grapefruit

2 grapefruits
2 sticks celery
½ beet (beetroot)

The earthy sweetness of the beet nicely balances the sharpness of white grapefruit, while the salty celery brings out all the flavours.

**NUTRIENTS**

Beta-carotene, folic acid, vitamin C;
calcium, magnesium, manganese,
phosphorus, potassium, sodium,
sulphur

| | |
|---|---|
| ENERGY | ★★★☆☆ |
| DETOX | ★★★★☆ |
| IMMUNITY | ★★☆☆☆ |
| DIGESTION | ★☆☆☆☆ |
| SKIN | ★★★☆☆ |

## 049 | tangy veggie

2 grapefruits
2 inches (5 cm) sweet potato
1 parsnip
1 stick celery

Another great combination of sweet, earthy root vegetables and sharp, white grapefruit, or pink if you prefer. The celery serves to magnify the flavours further.

**NUTRIENTS**

Beta-carotene, folic acid, vitamin C,
vitamin E; calcium, magnesium,
manganese, phosphorus, potassium,
sodium, sulphur

| | |
|---|---|
| ENERGY | ★★★☆☆ |
| DETOX | ★★★☆☆ |
| IMMUNITY | ★★☆☆☆ |
| DIGESTION | ★☆☆☆☆ |
| SKIN | ★★☆☆☆ |

## 050 | grapefruit cold zap

2 grapefruits
1 lemon
1 inch (2.5 cm) ginger root
1 clove garlic

You'd only really want this one if you were full of cold, unless you're trying to keep vampires away.

**NUTRIENTS**

Beta-carotene, folic acid, vitamin C;
calcium, magnesium, phosphorus,
potassium, sulphur

| | |
|---|---|
| ENERGY | ★★★☆☆ |
| DETOX | ★★☆☆☆ |
| IMMUNITY | ★★★★★ |
| DIGESTION | ★★☆☆☆ |
| SKIN | ★★★☆☆ |

## 051 | the original juice

4 oranges

Pure OJ is certainly the number one juice in the West, but not even the so-called "freshly squeezed" juices come close to making your own and drinking it immediately.

**NUTRIENTS**

Beta-carotene, vitamin C; calcium, magnesium, phosphorus, potassium

| | |
|---|---|
| ENERGY | ★★★★☆ |
| DETOX | ★☆☆☆☆ |
| IMMUNITY | ★★★★☆ |
| DIGESTION | ☆☆☆☆☆ |
| SKIN | ★★☆☆☆ |

## 052 | bloodthirst

6 blood oranges

A winter speciality, sweet, red blood oranges remind me of rare trips to my family home in Malta in the winter. You can often find them in supermarkets – particularly small, juicy organic ones. Best left unadulterated by other fruits.

**NUTRIENTS**

Beta-carotene, vitamin C; calcium, magnesium, phosphorus, potassium

| | |
|---|---|
| ENERGY | ★★★★☆ |
| DETOX | ★☆☆☆☆ |
| IMMUNITY | ★★★★☆ |
| DIGESTION | ☆☆☆☆☆ |
| SKIN | ★★☆☆☆ |

## 053 | orange basic

2 oranges
1 apple
3 carrots
1 stick celery
1 inch (2 cm) ginger root

One of my everyday staples – it doesn't require too much imagination as most refrigerators and fruit bowls will have the ingredients.

**NUTRIENTS**

Beta-carotene, folic acid, vitamin C; calcium, magnesium, manganese, phosphorus, potassium, sodium, sulphur

| | |
|---|---|
| ENERGY | ★★★★☆ |
| DETOX | ★★★★☆ |
| IMMUNITY | ★★★★☆ |
| DIGESTION | ★★☆☆☆ |
| SKIN | ★★★☆☆ |

## 054 | bright orange

2 oranges
4 carrots

Even easier than the Basic, the incredible colour of this simple
combination heralds an equally amazing taste.

**NUTRIENTS**

Beta-carotene, folic acid, vitamin C;
calcium, magnesium, phosphorus,
potassium, sodium, sulphur

| | |
|---|---|
| ENERGY | ★★★★☆ |
| DETOX | ★★★☆☆ |
| IMMUNITY | ★★★★☆ |
| DIGESTION | ★☆☆☆☆ |
| SKIN | ★★★☆☆ |

## 055 | florida blue

2 oranges
1 pink grapefruit
1 handful blueberries

If you use a sweet pink grapefruit,
rather than a sharper white one,
this blend is divine.

**NUTRIENTS**

Beta-carotene, biotin, folic acid,
vitamins B1, B2, B6, C and E; calcium,
magnesium, phosphorus, potassium,
sodium, sulphur

| | |
|---|---|
| ENERGY | ★★★★☆ |
| DETOX | ★☆☆☆☆ |
| IMMUNITY | ★★★★★ |
| DIGESTION | ★★☆☆☆ |
| SKIN | ★★★☆☆ |

# 056 | orange crudités

2 oranges
$\frac{1}{2}$ long cucumber
2 carrots
1 stick celery

The three vegetables in this juice gently dilute the sweet, sharp taste of oranges, and make it a lighter, more refreshing drink.

## NUTRIENTS

Beta-carotene, folic acid, vitamin C; calcium, magnesium, manganese, phosphorus, potassium, sodium, sulphur

ENERGY      ★★★☆☆
DETOX       ★★☆☆☆
IMMUNITY    ★★★☆☆
DIGESTION   ★★☆☆☆
SKIN        ★★★☆☆

# 057 | power packed c

3 oranges
1 guava
1 handful strawberries

With three of the richest sources of vitamin C mixed together, this is not only a delicious drink but is also a strong immune booster that helps keep illnesses at bay.

## NUTRIENTS

Beta-carotene, biotin, folic acid, vitamin B3, vitamin C; calcium, magnesium, phosphorus, potassium, sodium, sulphur

ENERGY      ★★★★★
DETOX       ★☆☆☆☆
IMMUNITY    ★★★★★
DIGESTION   ☆☆☆☆☆
SKIN        ★★★★☆

## 058 | william's orange

2 oranges
2 pears

You'd think the pears would get swamped by the oranges in this juice, but, in fact, they just tone down the tang beautifully. It's best to use a sweet variety of pear such as Williams.

### NUTRIENTS

Beta-carotene, folic acid, vitamin C; calcium, magnesium, phosphorus, potassium, sulphur

| | |
|---|---|
| ENERGY | ★★★★☆ |
| DETOX | ★☆☆☆☆ |
| IMMUNITY | ★★★☆☆ |
| DIGESTION | ★☆☆☆☆ |
| SKIN | ★☆☆☆☆ |

## 059 | orange medley

2 oranges
½ melon
1 nectarine

Use a cantaloupe melon to make this a wonderful blend of orange-coloured fruits.

### NUTRIENTS

Beta-carotene, folic acid, vitamin C; calcium, magnesium, phosphorus, potassium, sodium

| | |
|---|---|
| ENERGY | ★★★★★ |
| DETOX | ★☆☆☆☆ |
| IMMUNITY | ★★★★★ |
| DIGESTION | ★★☆☆☆ |
| SKIN | ★★★★☆ |

## 060 | citrus sweet

2 oranges
3 tangerines

This juice really highlights the differences between the tastes of oranges and the smaller tangerine or other similar fruits. Clementines or any small, easily peeled orange citrus fruits may be used.

### NUTRIENTS

Beta-carotene, folic acid, vitamin C; calcium, magnesium, phosphorus, potassium, sodium

| | |
|---|---|
| ENERGY | ★★★★☆ |
| DETOX | ★☆☆☆☆ |
| IMMUNITY | ★★★★☆ |
| DIGESTION | ☆☆☆☆☆ |
| SKIN | ☆☆☆☆☆ |

# 061 | biting orange

4 oranges
½ inch (1 cm) ginger root

Almost any juice goes well with ginger in my book, but this sweet orange with a ginger bite giving it a festive winter flavour is a particular favourite.

**NUTRIENTS**

Beta-carotene, vitamin C, calcium;
magnesium, phosphorus, potassium

| | |
|---|---|
| ENERGY | ★★★★☆ |
| DETOX | ☆☆☆☆☆ |
| IMMUNITY | ★★★★☆ |
| DIGESTION | ★★☆☆☆ |
| SKIN | ★☆☆☆☆ |

# 062 | bitter melon

2 oranges
2 thick slices of melon

Bitter Melon is actually the name of an Indian vegetable (and a 90s American rock band), but also sums up this juice's tangy twist on sweet melon. Use a cantaloupe or honeydew melon.

**NUTRIENTS**

Beta-carotene, folic acid, vitamin C;
calcium, magnesium, phosphorus,
potassium, sodium, sulphur

| | |
|---|---|
| ENERGY | ★★★★★ |
| DETOX | ★☆☆☆☆ |
| IMMUNITY | ★★★★★ |
| DIGESTION | ☆☆☆☆☆ |
| SKIN | ★★★★☆ |

# 063 | orange winter crumble

2 oranges
2 apples
1 handful blackberries

I love the blend of orange juice with the traditional winter mixture of apple and blackberry used in pies and crumbles.

**NUTRIENTS**

Beta-carotene, folic acid, vitamin C,
vitamin E; calcium, iron, magnesium,
manganese, phosphorus, potassium,
sodium, sulphur

| | |
|---|---|
| ENERGY | ★★★★★ |
| DETOX | ★★☆☆☆ |
| IMMUNITY | ★★★★★ |
| DIGESTION | ★☆☆☆☆ |
| SKIN | ★★★★☆ |

## 064 | citrus sharp

3 oranges
1 lemon
1 lime

The colour of this refreshing juice hails a tart
tickling of the tastebuds, and all that citrus fruit
gives you a great immune boost.

**NUTRIENTS**

Beta-carotene, folic acid, vitamin C;
calcium, magnesium, phosphorus,
potassium, sodium, sulphur

| | |
|---|---|
| ENERGY | ★★★★☆ |
| DETOX | ★☆☆☆☆ |
| IMMUNITY | ★★★★★ |
| DIGESTION | ☆☆☆☆☆ |
| SKIN | ★★☆☆☆ |

## 065 | muddy puddle

3 oranges
1 handful spinach
1 handful watercress
2 broccoli florets

The name of this originates from a drink a friend of mind used to have
at college – orange juice and cola. But it's a far cry from that in terms of
sweetness and health properties. The strength of flavour of the oranges
carries the earthy, strong taste of the greens.

**NUTRIENTS**

Beta-carotene, vitamin B5, vitamin C;
calcium, magnesium, phosphorus,
potassium, sodium

| | |
|---|---|
| ENERGY | ★★★☆☆ |
| DETOX | ★★★★☆ |
| IMMUNITY | ★★★☆☆ |
| DIGESTION | ★☆☆☆☆ |
| SKIN | ★★★☆☆ |

## 066 | blackcurrant twist

3 oranges
1 handful blackcurrants
¼ fennel bulb

This always reminds me of a tangy version of blackcurrant and aniseed
sweets I would buy as a child.

**NUTRIENTS**

Beta-carotene, biotin, vitamins B5,
C and E; calcium, magnesium,
phosphorus, potassium, sodium,
sulphur

| | |
|---|---|
| ENERGY | ★★★☆☆ |
| DETOX | ☆☆☆☆☆ |
| IMMUNITY | ★★★☆☆ |
| DIGESTION | ☆☆☆☆☆ |
| SKIN | ★★☆☆☆ |

## 067 | muddy tonic

4 oranges
1 teaspoon spirulina

I love the earthy green taste mixed with orange, although the brown
colour isn't the most appealing. It's best to shake the juice (or a portion
of it) with the spirulina in a jar so it doesn't go lumpy.

**NUTRIENTS**

Beta-carotene, vitamins B1, B3, B5,
B6 and C; calcium, iron, magnesium,
phosphorus, potassium, sodium;
protein, essential fatty acids

| | |
|---|---|
| ENERGY | ★★★☆☆ |
| DETOX | ★★★☆☆ |
| IMMUNITY | ★★☆☆☆ |
| DIGESTION | ☆☆☆☆☆ |
| SKIN | ★★☆☆☆ |

## 068 | bloody orange

3 oranges
1 beet (beetroot)

The name is a reference to this juice's thick red colour and not to blood
oranges which are, unfortunately, all too rare – the earthy taste of beet
cuts through the sharpness of good oranges well.

**NUTRIENTS**

Beta-carotene, folic acid, vitamin C;
calcium, magnesium, phosphorus,
potassium, sodium

| | |
|---|---|
| ENERGY | ★★★☆☆ |
| DETOX | ★★☆☆☆ |
| IMMUNITY | ★★★☆☆ |
| DIGESTION | ☆☆☆☆☆ |
| SKIN | ★★★☆☆ |

## 069 | orange aniseed twist

3 oranges
2 sticks celery
$\frac{1}{4}$ fennel bulb

The fennel gives a great turn to this recipe, while the saltiness of the celery brings out the flavours. All in all, very refreshing.

**NUTRIENTS**

Beta-carotene, folic acid, vitamin C; calcium, magnesium, manganese, phosphorus, potassium, sodium, sulphur

| | |
|---|---|
| ENERGY | ★★★☆☆ |
| DETOX | ★☆☆☆☆ |
| IMMUNITY | ★☆☆☆☆ |
| DIGESTION | ★★★☆☆ |
| SKIN | ★☆☆☆☆ |

## 070 | water cooler II

3 oranges
1 thick slice watermelon

Unbelievably light and refreshing, the watermelon takes the edge off the tangy orange.

**NUTRIENTS**

Beta-carotene, vitamin C; calcium, iron, magnesium, phosphorus, potassium, sodium, sulphur

| | |
|---|---|
| ENERGY | ★★★★☆ |
| DETOX | ★★☆☆☆ |
| IMMUNITY | ★★★☆☆ |
| DIGESTION | ☆☆☆☆☆ |
| SKIN | ★★★★☆ |

## 071 | orange pepper

3 oranges
$\frac{1}{2}$ red or yellow bell pepper
1 kale leaf
1 handful watercress

The strong taste of oranges carries the more subtle tastes of the vegetables in this juice. Don't be put off by the muddy colour.

**NUTRIENTS**

Beta-carotene, folic acid, vitamins B3, C and E; calcium, iron, magnesium, manganese, phosphorus, potassium, sodium, sulphur

| | |
|---|---|
| ENERGY | ★★☆☆☆ |
| DETOX | ★★★☆☆ |
| IMMUNITY | ★★★☆☆ |
| DIGESTION | ★★☆☆☆ |
| SKIN | ★★★★☆ |

## 072 | orange blush

3 oranges
1 apple
1 handful raspberries

A tangy pink juice which blends
three fantastic fruits perfectly –
definitely greater than the sum
of its parts.

**NUTRIENTS**
Beta-carotene, biotin, folic acid,
vitamin C; calcium, magnesium,
manganese, phosphorus,
potassium, sodium, sulphur

ENERGY ★★★★★
DETOX ★☆☆☆☆
IMMUNITY ★★★☆☆
DIGESTION ★☆☆☆☆
SKIN ★★★☆☆

## 073 | counteractor

3 oranges
¼ red cabbage
¼ inch (0.5 cm) ginger root

Some people find oranges too acidic on their digestion – here the
soothing cabbage and ginger provide the perfect balance.

**NUTRIENTS**
Beta-carotene, folic acid, vitamin C,
vitamin E; calcium, magnesium,
phosphorus, potassium, sodium

ENERGY ★★★☆☆
DETOX ★☆☆☆☆
IMMUNITY ★★☆☆☆
DIGESTION ★★★☆☆
SKIN ★★☆☆☆

## 074 | pure raspberry

2 large handfuls raspberries

For the vast majority of us an absurd luxury, so make just a small glassful and savour every drop.

**NUTRIENTS**

Beta-carotene, biotin, vitamin C; calcium, magnesium, manganese, phosphorus, potassium, sodium, sulphur

| | |
|---|---|
| ENERGY | ★★★★★ |
| DETOX | ★☆☆☆☆ |
| IMMUNITY | ★★★☆☆ |
| DIGESTION | ☆☆☆☆☆ |
| SKIN | ★★★☆☆ |

## 075 | raspapple

2 large handfuls raspberries
2 large apples

A simple but splendid blend of juices.

**NUTRIENTS**

Beta-carotene, biotin, folic acid, vitamin C; calcium, magnesium, manganese, phosphorus, potassium, sodium, sulphur

| | |
|---|---|
| ENERGY | ★★★★★ |
| DETOX | ★☆☆☆☆ |
| IMMUNITY | ★★☆☆☆ |
| DIGESTION | ★☆☆☆☆ |
| SKIN | ★★★☆☆ |

## 076 | raspapple tang

2 large handfuls raspberries
2 large apples
1 lime

Remarkably different with just the addition of a little lime.

**NUTRIENTS**

Beta-carotene, biotin, folic acid, vitamin C; calcium, magnesium, manganese, phosphorus, potassium, sodium, sulphur

| | |
|---|---|
| ENERGY | ★★★★☆ |
| DETOX | ★☆☆☆☆ |
| IMMUNITY | ★★★★☆ |
| DIGESTION | ★☆☆☆☆ |
| SKIN | ★★☆☆☆ |

## 077 | citrusberry

2 large handfuls raspberries
2 large oranges
1 tangerine

This is such a classic, delicious blend, they even sell it in supermarkets without the tangerine, which I find just tones it down a nice touch.

**NUTRIENTS**

Beta-carotene, biotin, vitamin C;
calcium, magnesium, manganese,
phosphorus, potassium, sodium, sulphur

| | |
|---|---|
| ENERGY | ★★★★★ |
| DETOX | ★☆☆☆☆ |
| IMMUNITY | ★★★★☆ |
| DIGESTION | ☆☆☆☆☆ |
| SKIN | ★★★☆☆ |

## 078 | sharp citrusberry

2 large handfuls raspberries
1 grapefruit
$\frac{1}{2}$ lemon

I almost prefer this one to the orange blend (see above), with the bite of the grapefruit and the nose-curling lemon.

**NUTRIENTS**

Beta-carotene, folic acid, biotin,
vitamin C; calcium, magnesium,
manganese, phosphorus, potassium,
sodium, sulphur

| | |
|---|---|
| ENERGY | ★★★★☆ |
| DETOX | ★☆☆☆☆ |
| IMMUNITY | ★★★☆☆ |
| DIGESTION | ☆☆☆☆☆ |
| SKIN | ★★★☆☆ |

## 079 | creamy raspberry

2 large handfuls raspberries
$\frac{1}{2}$ melon
1 stick celery

With the creaminess of the melon, you'd think you were drinking more than just fruit juice, while the salty celery lifts all the flavours.

**NUTRIENTS**

Beta-carotene, biotin, folic acid,
vitamin C; calcium, magnesium,
manganese, phosphorus, potassium,
sodium, sulphur

| | |
|---|---|
| ENERGY | ★★★★★ |
| DETOX | ★☆☆☆☆ |
| IMMUNITY | ★★★☆☆ |
| DIGESTION | ☆☆☆☆☆ |
| SKIN | ★★★★☆ |

## 080 | gently raspberry

2 large handfuls raspberries
2 pears
$\frac{1}{4}$ cucumber

Not quite as strange a combination as you may initially think – the cucumber in this appears to save the pears from being drowned out by the raspberries.

**NUTRIENTS**

Beta-carotene, biotin, folic acid,
vitamin C; calcium, magnesium,
manganese, phosphorus, potassium,
sodium, sulphur

| | |
|---|---|
| ENERGY | ★★★☆☆ |
| DETOX | ★☆☆☆☆ |
| IMMUNITY | ★★☆☆☆ |
| DIGESTION | ★☆☆☆☆ |
| SKIN | ★★☆☆☆ |

## 081 | raspberry sensation

2 large handfuls raspberries
$\frac{1}{2}$ pineapple

A truly sensational combination – go on, spoil yourself with two independently rich fruits laden with goodness.

**NUTRIENTS**

Beta-carotene, biotin, folic acid, vitamin C;
calcium, magnesium, manganese phosphorus,
potassium, sodium, sulphur

| | |
|---|---|
| ENERGY | ★★★★★ |
| DETOX | ★☆☆☆☆ |
| IMMUNITY | ★★☆☆☆ |
| DIGESTION | ★★★★☆ |
| SKIN | ★★★☆☆ |

## 082 | berry bonanza

2 large handfuls raspberries
1 handful blackcurrants
1 handful blueberries

Taking the luxury even
further …this berry combination
is a blessing to your tastebuds
and your body.

**NUTRIENTS**

Beta-carotene, biotin, folic acid,
vitamins B1, B2, B5, B6, C and E;
calcium, chromium, magnesium,
phosphorus, potassium, sodium,
sulphur

| | |
|---|---|
| ENERGY | ★★★★★ |
| DETOX | ★☆☆☆☆ |
| IMMUNITY | ★★★★★ |
| DIGESTION | ☆☆☆☆☆ |
| SKIN | ★★★★☆ |

## 083 | morning berry basic

2 large handfuls raspberries
2 apples
1 orange
1 teaspoon spirulina

Fruit bowl classics with the raspberries and some spirulina for an
extra health kick. To avoid green lumps, shake the spirulina in a jar
with a little of the juice before mixing it in with the rest.

**NUTRIENTS**

Beta-carotene, vitamins B1, B3, B5, B6 and C;
calcium, iron, magnesium, manganese,
phosphorus, potassium, sodium, sulphur;
protein, essential fatty acids

| | |
|---|---|
| ENERGY | ★★★★☆ |
| DETOX | ★★★★☆ |
| IMMUNITY | ★★★☆☆ |
| DIGESTION | ★☆☆☆☆ |
| SKIN | ★★★★☆ |

## 084 | pure peach

4 peaches or nectarines

Pure heaven for anyone with the slightest penchant for fruit
of any sort.

**NUTRIENTS**

Beta-carotene, folic acid, vitamin B3,
vitamin C; calcium, magnesium, phosphorus,
potassium, sodium, sulphur

| | |
|---|---|
| ENERGY | ★★★★★ |
| DETOX | ★☆☆☆☆ |
| IMMUNITY | ★★★★☆ |
| DIGESTION | ★★☆☆☆ |
| SKIN | ★★★★☆ |

## 085 | eve's peach

2 peaches or nectarines
2 apples

I'm sure the serpent would not have had to do much persuading
for this one!

**NUTRIENTS**

Beta-carotene, folic acid, vitamin B3,
vitamin C; calcium, magnesium, phosphorus,
potassium, sodium, sulphur

| | |
|---|---|
| ENERGY | ★★★★★ |
| DETOX | ★☆☆☆☆ |
| IMMUNITY | ★★★★☆ |
| DIGESTION | ★★☆☆☆ |
| SKIN | ★★★★☆ |

## 086 | peach 'n' pine

2 peaches or nectarines
½ pineapple

Tropical and temperate, tangy and delicate.

**NUTRIENTS**

Beta-carotene, folic acid, vitamin B3,
vitamin C; calcium, magnesium,
manganese, phosphorus, potassium,
sodium, sulphur

| | |
|---|---|
| ENERGY | ★★★★★ |
| DETOX | ★☆☆☆☆ |
| IMMUNITY | ★★★☆☆ |
| DIGESTION | ★★★☆☆ |
| SKIN | ★★★☆☆ |

# 087 | black peach

2 peaches or nectarines
2 handfuls blueberries, blackberries and/or blackcurrants

A summer delight – each drop to be savoured. Play with the different berry combinations to change the flavour and the sweetness.

### NUTRIENTS

Beta-carotene, biotin, folic acid, vitamins B1, B2, B3, B6, C and E; calcium, chromium, iron, magnesium, manganese, phosphorus, potassium, sodium, sulphur

| | |
|---|---|
| ENERGY | ★★★★★ |
| DETOX | ★★☆☆☆ |
| IMMUNITY | ★★★★☆ |
| DIGESTION | ★☆☆☆☆ |
| SKIN | ★★★★★ |

# 088 | pink peach

2 peaches or nectarines
2 handfuls strawberries and raspberries

Another exquisite summer luxury – choose your favourite combination.

### NUTRIENTS

Beta-carotene, biotin, folic acid, vitamin B3, vitamin C; calcium, magnesium, phosphorus, potassium, sodium, sulphur

| | |
|---|---|
| ENERGY | ★★★★★ |
| DETOX | ★★☆☆☆ |
| IMMUNITY | ★★★★☆ |
| DIGESTION | ★☆☆☆☆ |
| SKIN | ★★★★★ |

# 089 | peaches and cream

2 peaches or nectarines
$\frac{1}{2}$ melon

If any creamless drink comes close to peaches and cream this delicious concoction is it.

### NUTRIENTS

Beta-carotene, folic acid, vitamin B3, vitamin C; calcium, magnesium, phosphorus, potassium, sodium, sulphur

| | |
|---|---|
| ENERGY | ★★★★★ |
| DETOX | ★☆☆☆☆ |
| IMMUNITY | ★★★★☆ |
| DIGESTION | ★☆☆☆☆ |
| SKIN | ★★★★☆ |

## 090 | minty peach

3 peaches or nectarines
1 apple
1 lime
1 small bunch fresh mint

One of the most refreshing combinations possible,
blended with the nectar of peaches.

**NUTRIENTS**

Beta-carotene, folic acid, vitamin B3,
vitamin C; calcium, magnesium,
phosphorus, potassium, sodium, sulphur

| | |
|---|---|
| ENERGY | ★★★★☆ |
| DETOX | ★☆☆☆☆ |
| IMMUNITY | ★★☆☆☆ |
| DIGESTION | ★★☆☆☆ |
| SKIN | ★★★★☆ |

## 091 | peaches and green

3 peaches or nectarines
2 sticks celery
1 teaspoon spirulina

Even the less inviting earthiness of the celery and spirulina are forgotten
in this super-healthy blend. To avoid green lumps, shake the spirulina in
a jar with a little of the juice before mixing it in with the rest.

**NUTRIENTS**

Beta-carotene, folic acid, vitamin B3,
vitamin C; calcium, magnesium, manganese,
phosphorus, potassium, sodium, sulphur;
protein, essential fatty acids

| | |
|---|---|
| ENERGY | ★★★☆☆ |
| DETOX | ★★★★☆ |
| IMMUNITY | ★★☆☆☆ |
| DIGESTION | ★☆☆☆☆ |
| SKIN | ★★★★☆ |

## 092 | tangerine cream

3 peaches or nectarines
2 tangerines or clementines

When oranges simply won't do – only the delicate taste of tangerine
or any similar citrus fruit. Combine with peach or nectarine and you
get a creamy, sweet blend.

### NUTRIENTS

Beta-carotene, folic acid, vitamin B3,
vitamin C; calcium, magnesium, phosphorus,
potassium, sodium, sulphur

| | |
|---|---|
| ENERGY | ★★★★★ |
| DETOX | ★☆☆☆☆ |
| IMMUNITY | ★★★★★ |
| DIGESTION | ★☆☆☆☆ |
| SKIN | ★★★★☆ |

## 093 | sunset peach

2 peaches or nectarines
1 apple
2 carrots
1 handful raspberries

The carrots add a surprising creamy sweetness to this
one and can even make up for getting a dud batch of
raspberries that aren't that sweet.

### NUTRIENTS

Beta-carotene, biotin, folic acid,
vitamin B3, vitamin C; calcium, magnesium,
manganese, phosphorus, potassium,
sodium, sulphur

| | |
|---|---|
| ENERGY | ★★★★★ |
| DETOX | ★★☆☆☆ |
| IMMUNITY | ★★★★★ |
| DIGESTION | ★★☆☆☆ |
| SKIN | ★★★★☆ |

## 094 | cherry pie

2 large handfuls cherries
2 apples

Nothing to do with pies at all, but the sweetness of apples blends beautifully with the cherries.

### NUTRIENTS

Beta-carotene, folic acid, vitamin C;
calcium, magnesium, phosphorus,
potassium, sodium, sulphur

| | |
|---|---|
| ENERGY | ★★★★★ |
| DETOX | ★★★☆☆ |
| IMMUNITY | ★★★★☆ |
| DIGESTION | ★★☆☆☆ |
| SKIN | ★★★☆☆ |

## 095 | citrus cherry

2 large handfuls cherries
2 oranges
½ lime

You'll be hard pressed to enjoy a better combination with orange juice as this one.

### NUTRIENTS

Beta-carotene, folic acid, vitamin C;
calcium, magnesium, phosphorus,
potassium, sodium, sulphur

| | |
|---|---|
| ENERGY | ★★★★★ |
| DETOX | ★☆☆☆☆ |
| IMMUNITY | ★★★★☆ |
| DIGESTION | ★☆☆☆☆ |
| SKIN | ★★★★☆ |

## 096 | sweet cherry pine

2 large handfuls cherries
½ pineapple

The combination of these two fruits produces an unbelievable sensation of intense taste and texture with the rich sweetness of the cherries and the pineapple's tang.

### NUTRIENTS

Beta-carotene, folic acid, vitamin C;
calcium, magnesium, manganese,
phosphorus, potassium, sodium, sulphur

| | |
|---|---|
| ENERGY | ★★★★☆ |
| DETOX | ★★☆☆☆ |
| IMMUNITY | ★★★★☆ |
| DIGESTION | ★★★☆☆ |
| SKIN | ★★★★☆ |

## 097 | thicker than water

2 large handfuls cherries
2 apples
$\frac{1}{2}$ beet (beetroot)

The colour of this smooth, sumptuous juice almost makes you
want to hold it as though it were a soft, pink velvet.

**NUTRIENTS**
Beta-carotene, folic acid,
vitamin C; calcium,
magnesium, phosphorus,
potassium, sodium, sulphur

| | |
|---|---|
| ENERGY | ★★★★★ |
| DETOX | ★★★☆☆ |
| IMMUNITY | ★★★★☆ |
| DIGESTION | ★★★☆☆ |
| SKIN | ★★★★☆ |

## 098 | cherry cooler

2 large handfuls cherries
$\frac{1}{2}$ long cucumber
2 sticks celery

This may seem like a peculiar combination but the cucumber and celery
provide delicious light relief from the density of the cherry juice.

**NUTRIENTS**
Beta-carotene, folic acid, vitamin C;
calcium, magnesium, manganese,
phosphorus, potassium, sodium, sulphur

| | |
|---|---|
| ENERGY | ★★★☆☆ |
| DETOX | ★★☆☆☆ |
| IMMUNITY | ★★★☆☆ |
| DIGESTION | ★★☆☆☆ |
| SKIN | ★★☆☆☆ |

## 099 | pure pear

4 pears

In addition to some of the tropical fruits, I think a ripe Williams pear ranks right up there as one of my favourites.

**NUTRIENTS**

Beta-carotene, folic acid, vitamin C; calcium, magnesium, phosphorus, potassium, sulphur

| | |
|---|---|
| ENERGY | ★★★★☆ |
| DETOX | ★★☆☆☆ |
| IMMUNITY | ★☆☆☆☆ |
| DIGESTION | ★★★☆☆ |
| SKIN | ★★☆☆☆ |

## 100 | pear basic

2 pears
1 apple
2 carrots
½ inch (1 cm) ginger root

A good, standard morning blend to set you up for the day ahead.

**NUTRIENTS**

Beta-carotene, folic acid, vitamin C; calcium, magnesium, phosphorus, potassium, sodium, sulphur

| | |
|---|---|
| ENERGY | ★★★★☆ |
| DETOX | ★★★☆☆ |
| IMMUNITY | ★★★☆☆ |
| DIGESTION | ★★☆☆☆ |
| SKIN | ★★★☆☆ |

## 101 | pear tart

4 pears
½ inch (1 cm) ginger root
¼ teaspoon ground cinnamon powder

Pears go so well with a gentle hint of spices. The ground cinnamon is best shaken up with the juice in a jar after it's made.

**NUTRIENTS**

Beta-carotene, folic acid, vitamin C; calcium, magnesium, phosphorus, potassium, sulphur

| | |
|---|---|
| ENERGY | ★★★★☆ |
| DETOX | ★☆☆☆☆ |
| IMMUITY | ★★★☆☆ |
| DIGESTION | ★★★☆☆ |
| SKIN | ★☆☆☆☆ |

# 102 | blue pear

2 pears
1 handful blueberries
1 handful blackberries

The sweetness of all three of these fruits is divine.

**NUTRIENTS**

Beta-carotene, biotin, folic acid,
vitamins B1, B2, B6, C, E; calcium,
chromium, iron, magnesium,
manganese, phosphorus, potassium,
sodium, sulphur

| | |
|---|---|
| ENERGY | ★★★★☆ |
| DETOX | ★★★☆☆ |
| IMMUNITY | ★★★★☆ |
| DIGESTION | ★☆☆☆☆ |
| SKIN | ★★★☆☆ |

# 103 | black pear

3 pears
1 handful blackcurrants

Quite distinct from Blue Pear, the sweet sharpness of the blackcurrants
blends wonderfully with pears.

**NUTRIENTS**

Beta-carotene, folic acid, biotin,
vitamins B5, C and E; calcium,
magnesium, phosphorus, potassium,
sodium, sulphur

| | |
|---|---|
| ENERGY | ★★★★☆ |
| DETOX | ★★★☆☆ |
| IMMUNITY | ★★★★☆ |
| DIGESTION | ★☆☆☆☆ |
| SKIN | ★★★☆☆ |

# 104 | pink pear

2 pears
1 handful raspberries
1 handful strawberries

In my view, raspberries and strawberries go well with pretty much
any fruit, and this is certainly no exception.

**NUTRIENTS**

Beta-carotene, biotin, folic acid,
vitamin C; calcium, magnesium,
manganese, phosphorus, potassium,
sodium, sulphur

| | |
|---|---|
| ENERGY | ★★★★★ |
| DETOX | ★★☆☆☆ |
| IMMUNITY | ★★★★☆ |
| DIGESTION | ★☆☆☆☆ |
| SKIN | ★★★☆☆ |

## 105 | pink pear II

3 pears
1 handful cranberries

Another bright pink juice, this one is fantastic for the immune system, particularly for urinary-tract infections. Unless you want a very sharp taste, make sure you use nearly ripe Williams pears.

**NUTRIENTS**

Beta-carotene, folic acid, vitamin C; calcium, iron, magnesium, phosphorus, potassium, sodium, sulphur

| | |
|---|---|
| ENERGY | ★★★☆☆ |
| DETOX | ★★☆☆☆ |
| IMMUNITY | ★★★★☆ |
| DIGESTION | ★☆☆☆☆ |
| SKIN | ★★★☆☆ |

## 106 | tangerine dream

3 pears
2 tangerines

Although pears go well with any citrus fruit, the slightly more delicate flavour of tangerine or clementine really draws out the taste of the pear.

**NUTRIENTS**

Beta-carotene, folic acid, vitamin C; calcium, magnesium, phosphorus, potassium, sodium, sulphur

| | |
|---|---|
| ENERGY | ★★★★☆ |
| DETOX | ★★☆☆☆ |
| IMMUNITY | ★★★☆☆ |
| DIGESTION | ★☆☆☆☆ |
| SKIN | ★★★☆☆ |

## 107 | big c pear

2 pears
2 kiwis
2 guavas

These two vitamin C-packed fruits create a divine taste with pear.

**NUTRIENTS**

Beta-carotene, folic acid, vitamin B3, vitamin C; calcium, magnesium, phosphorus, potassium, sodium, sulphur

| | |
|---|---|
| ENERGY | ★★★★★ |
| DETOX | ★★☆☆☆ |
| IMMUNITY | ★★★★★ |
| DIGESTION | ★★☆☆☆ |
| SKIN | ★★★★☆ |

## 108 | creamy pear

3 pears
1 thick slice melon
1 small bunch fresh mint

The taste and texture of melon juice somehow conjures up the sensation of creaminess.

### NUTRIENTS

Beta-carotene, folic acid, vitamin C;
calcium, magnesium, phosphorus,
potassium, sodium, sulphur

| | |
|---|---|
| ENERGY | ★★★★☆ |
| DETOX | ★☆☆☆☆ |
| IMMUNITY | ★★★★☆ |
| DIGESTION | ★★☆☆☆ |
| SKIN | ★★★☆☆ |

## 109 | tropical pear

3 pears
$\frac{1}{4}$ pineapple
$\frac{1}{2}$ lime

Perhaps two of my favourite fruits with a hint of tangy lime.

### NUTRIENTS

Beta-carotene, folic acid, vitamin C;
calcium, magnesium, manganese,
phosphorus, potassium, sodium,
sulphur

| | |
|---|---|
| ENERGY | ★★★★☆ |
| DETOX | ★★☆☆☆ |
| IMMUNITY | ★★★★☆ |
| DIGESTION | ★★★☆☆ |
| SKIN | ★★☆☆☆ |

## 110 | pear dream

3 pears
4 apricots

Two delicate, gentle flavours bound to create a dreamy combination.

### NUTRIENTS

Beta-carotene, folic acid, vitamin C;
calcium, magnesium, phosphorus,
potassium, sulphur

| | |
|---|---|
| ENERGY | ★★★★☆ |
| DETOX | ★★☆☆☆ |
| IMMUNITY | ★★★★☆ |
| DIGESTION | ★★☆☆☆ |
| SKIN | ★★★★☆ |

## 111 | breakfast pear

3 pears
2 sticks celery
$\frac{1}{2}$ inch (1 cm) ginger root

The saltiness of celery and the hot bite of the ginger make this
a great morning recipe for awakening the tastebuds.

### NUTRIENTS

| | | |
|---|---|---|
| Beta-carotene, folic acid, vitamin C; | ENERGY | ★★★☆☆ |
| calcium, magnesium, phosphorus, | DETOX | ★★★★☆ |
| potassium, sodium, sulphur | IMMUNITY | ★★★☆☆ |
| | DIGESTION | ★★☆☆☆ |
| | SKIN | ★☆☆☆☆ |

## 112 | fresh pear

3 pears
$\frac{1}{2}$ long cucumber
small bunch fresh mint

There aren't many juices like that of a cucumber to quench your
thirst and combined with pear and then the mint too … mmm.

### NUTRIENTS

| | | |
|---|---|---|
| Beta-carotene, folic acid, vitamin C; | ENERGY | ★★★☆☆ |
| calcium, magnesium, phosphorus, | DETOX | ★★★★☆ |
| potassium, sodium, sulphur | IMMUNITY | ★☆☆☆☆ |
| | DIGESTION | ★★☆☆☆ |
| | SKIN | ★★☆☆☆ |

## 113 | gut soother

2 pears
2 carrots
$\frac{1}{2}$ pineapple
$\frac{1}{2}$ inch (1 cm) ginger root

The blend of these three along with the ginger not only make
a great taste, but they're good for the digestive tract too.

### NUTRIENTS

| | | |
|---|---|---|
| Beta-carotene, folic acid, vitamin C; | ENERGY | ★★★☆☆ |
| calcium, magnesium, manganese, | DETOX | ★★☆☆☆ |
| phosphorus, potassium, sodium, | IMMUNITY | ★★★☆☆ |
| sulphur | DIGESTION | ★★★★★ |
| | SKIN | ★★★☆☆ |

# 114 | pure pineapple

1 pineapple

It was always my favourite juice in a can, bottle or carton … until
I discovered the real thing.

**NUTRIENTS**

Beta-carotene, folic acid, vitamin C;
calcium, magnesium, manganese,
phosphorus, potassium, sodium

| | |
|---|---|
| ENERGY | ★★★★★ |
| DETOX | ★★★☆☆ |
| IMMUNITY | ★★★☆☆ |
| DIGESTION | ★★★★★ |
| SKIN | ★★★☆☆ |

# 115 | pineapple tang

1 pineapple
1 lime

Mixed with lime, pineapple takes me straight to the streets of Bangkok.

**NUTRIENTS**

Beta-carotene, folic acid, vitamin C;
calcium, magnesium, manganese,
phosphorus, potassium, sodium,
sulphur

| | |
|---|---|
| ENERGY | ★★★★★ |
| DETOX | ★★★☆☆ |
| IMMUNITY | ★★★☆☆ |
| DIGESTION | ★★★★★ |
| SKIN | ★★★☆☆ |

# 116 | pink pineapple

$\frac{1}{2}$ pineapple
1 handful raspberries
1 handful strawberries

This rich yet fresh juice is a beautiful shade of pink created by a blend
of tropical and temperate climes.

**NUTRIENTS**

Beta-carotene, biotin, folic acid,
vitamin C; calcium, magnesium,
manganese, phosphorus, potassium,
sodium, sulphur

| | |
|---|---|
| ENERGY | ★★★★★ |
| DETOX | ★☆☆☆☆ |
| IMMUNITY | ★★★★☆ |
| DIGESTION | ★★★☆☆ |
| SKIN | ★★★☆☆ |

## 117 | black pineapple

½ pineapple
1 handful blackcurrants
1 handful blackberries

Another tropic-temperate blend of fruits which goes down perfectly.

**NUTRIENTS**

Beta-carotene, biotin, folic acid,
vitamins B5, C and E; calcium, iron,
magnesium, manganese, phosphorus,
potassium, sodium, sulphur

| | |
|---|---|
| ENERGY | ★★★★★ |
| DETOX | ★★☆☆☆ |
| IMMUNITY | ★★★★☆ |
| DIGESTION | ★★★☆☆ |
| SKIN | ★★★★☆ |

## 118 | sweet sunset

½ pineapple
1 thick slice watermelon

The watery sweetness of the melon contrasts ideally with the rich tang
of pineapple in this all-round health-affirming, thirst-quenching drink.

**NUTRIENTS**

Beta-carotene, folic acid, vitamin B5,
vitamin C; calcium, magnesium,
manganese, phosphorus, potassium,
sodium

| | |
|---|---|
| ENERGY | ★★★★★ |
| DETOX | ★★★☆☆ |
| IMMUNITY | ★★★★☆ |
| DIGESTION | ★★☆☆☆ |
| SKIN | ★★★★☆ |

## 119 | aniseed black

½ pineapple
1 large handful blackcurrants
½ fennel bulb

A stark reminder of blackcurrant and aniseed boiled candy with
a tangy difference.

**NUTRIENTS**

Beta-carotene, biotin, folic acid,
vitamins B5, C and E; calcium,
magnesium, manganese, phosphorus,
potassium, sodium, sulphur

| | |
|---|---|
| ENERGY | ★★★★☆ |
| DETOX | ★☆☆☆☆ |
| IMMUNITY | ★★★☆☆ |
| DIGESTION | ★★★★☆ |
| SKIN | ★★★★☆ |

# 120 | ginger zinger

½ pineapple
2 oranges
1 inch (2.5 cm) ginger root

One of the most refreshing, tangy combinations there is. You could add more ginger if you're a real fan and get an even greater boost from this all-round wonder food.

**NUTRIENTS**

Beta-carotene, folic acid, vitamin C; calcium, magnesium, manganese, phosphorus, potassium, sodium

| | |
|---|---|
| ENERGY | ★★★★☆ |
| DETOX | ★☆☆☆☆ |
| IMMUNITY | ★★★★☆ |
| DIGESTION | ★★★☆☆ |
| SKIN | ★★☆☆☆ |

# 121 | pineapple basic

½ pineapple
1 apple
3 carrots
1 stick celery

As long as you have the actual pineapple, this is a simple mixture of ingredients you're likely to have in your fruit bowl and refrigerator, and one which turns out a delicious morning juice.

**NUTRIENTS**

Beta-carotene, folic acid, vitamin C; calcium, magnesium, manganese, phosphorus, potassium, sodium, sulphur

| | |
|---|---|
| ENERGY | ★★★★☆ |
| DETOX | ★★★★☆ |
| IMMUNITY | ★★★★☆ |
| DIGESTION | ★★★★☆ |
| SKIN | ★★★☆☆ |

# 122 | muddy pine

1 pineapple
1 teaspoon spirulina powder

The tangy, strong taste of the pineapple easily
carries the earthy goodness of the spirulina. Best
to shake a bit of the juice with the spirulina in a
jar and then mix it all up to avoid getting lumps
of green powder.

**NUTRIENTS**

Beta-carotene, folic acid, vitamins B1,
B3, B5, B6 and C; calcium, iron,
magnesium, manganese, phosphorus,
potassium, sodium; protein,
essential fatty acids

| | |
|---|---|
| ENERGY | ★★★★★ |
| DETOX | ★★★★★ |
| IMMUNITY | ★★★☆☆ |
| DIGESTION | ★★★★☆ |
| SKIN | ★★★★☆ |

# 123 | aniseed twist

$\frac{1}{2}$ pineapple
2 apples
$\frac{1}{2}$ fennel bulb

The fennel comes as an unexpected twist against the pineapple
and apple. A delicious afternoon pick-me-up.

**NUTRIENTS**

Beta-carotene, folic acid, vitamin C;
calcium, magnesium, manganese,
phosphorus, potassium, sodium,
sulphur

| | |
|---|---|
| ENERGY | ★★★★☆ |
| DETOX | ★★★☆☆ |
| IMMUNITY | ★★★☆☆ |
| DIGESTION | ★★★★☆ |
| SKIN | ★★★☆☆ |

## 124 | bloody pineapple

½ pineapple
1 beet (beetroot)

Another mixture where the powerful taste of pineapple carries a flavour
that some people find too earthy in other combinations.

**NUTRIENTS**

Beta-carotene, folic acid, vitamin C;
calcium, magnesium, manganese,
phosphorus, potassium, sodium

| | |
|---|---|
| ENERGY | ★★★★☆ |
| DETOX | ★★★★☆ |
| IMMUNITY | ★★★☆☆ |
| DIGESTION | ★★★★☆ |
| SKIN | ★★★★☆ |

## 125 | green pines

½ pineapple
3 sticks celery
1 large handful watercress

This is a very cleansing juice with rich, peppery undertones supplied
by the watercress.

**NUTRIENTS**

Beta-carotene, folic acid, vitamin C,
vitamin E; calcium, iron, magnesium,
manganese, phosphorus, potassium,
sodium, sulphur

| | |
|---|---|
| ENERGY | ★★★☆☆ |
| DETOX | ★★★★☆ |
| IMMUNITY | ★★★☆☆ |
| DIGESTION | ★★★☆☆ |
| SKIN | ★★★★☆ |

## 126 | digestaid

½ pineapple
1 thick slice white cabbage
1 inch (2.5 cm) ginger root
1 small bunch fresh mint

Pineapple contains bromelain (a natural substance that helps digestion),
cabbage soothes the stomach lining and ginger calms the digestive tract –
an all-round gut tonic.

**NUTRIENTS**

Beta-carotene, folic acid, vitamin C,
vitamin E; calcium, magnesium,
manganese, phosphorus, potassium,
sodium

| | |
|---|---|
| ENERGY | ★★★☆☆ |
| DETOX | ★★★☆☆ |
| IMMUNITY | ★★☆☆☆ |
| DIGESTION | ★★★★★ |
| SKIN | ★★★☆☆ |

## 127 | joint aid

1 pineapple
2 inches (5 cm) ginger root
1 tablespoon (15 ml) flaxseed (linseed) oil

The bromelain in pineapple can help reduce inflammation, as can ginger
and the essential fatty acids in flax oil. Two inches of ginger is a pretty
hefty dose, so reduce it if you find it too strong.

### NUTRIENTS

Beta-carotene, folic acid, vitamin C;
calcium, magnesium, manganese, phosphorus,
potassium, sodium; essential fatty acids

| | |
|---|---|
| ENERGY | ★★★★★ |
| DETOX | ★★★☆☆ |
| IMMUNITY | ★★★★★ |
| DIGESTION | ★★★★☆ |
| SKIN | ★★★★☆ |

## 128 | pineapple magic

½ pineapple
1 thick slice of melon
2 guavas

This exquisite combination of three flavoursome fruits
creates a creamy, magical taste which is also very rich
in immunity-boosting nutrients.

### NUTRIENTS

Beta-carotene, folic acid,
vitamin B3, vitamin C; calcium,
magnesium, manganese, phosphorus,
potassium, sodium, sulphur

| | |
|---|---|
| ENERGY | ★★★★★ |
| DETOX | ★★☆☆☆ |
| IMMUNITY | ★★★★★ |
| DIGESTION | ★★★☆☆ |
| SKIN | ★★★☆☆ |

## 129 | what's up doc?

5 carrots

The original basic vegetable juice, this is pure orange, creamy and vibrant, and probably the most popular and palatable of all the solo vegetable juices.

**NUTRIENTS**

Beta-carotene, folic acid, vitamin C; calcium, magnesium, phosphorus, potassium, sodium, sulphur

| | |
|---|---|
| ENERGY | ★★★★☆ |
| DETOX | ★★★★☆ |
| IMMUNITY | ★★★★☆ |
| DIGESTION | ★★☆☆☆ |
| SKIN | ★★★★★ |

## 130 | easy morning

3 carrots
1 apple
½ orange
1 stick celery
½ inch (1 cm) ginger root

This is my absolute staple – when I'm not feeling any more adventurous, this is what pours daily from my juicer. It makes an invigorating start to any day.

**NUTRIENTS**

Beta-carotene, folic acid, vitamin C; calcium, magnesium, manganese, phosphorus, potassium, sodium, sulphur

| | |
|---|---|
| ENERGY | ★★★★☆ |
| DETOX | ★★★☆☆ |
| IMMUNITY | ★★★☆☆ |
| DIGESTION | ★★☆☆☆ |
| SKIN | ★★★☆☆ |

## 131 | apple basic

4 carrots
1 apple

Most refrigerators will house a couple of carrots and most fruit
bowls an apple, so this is a good, basic standby for any morning.

**NUTRIENTS**

Beta-carotene, folic acid, vitamin C;

calcium, magnesium, phosphorus,

potassium, sodium, sulphur

| | |
|---|---|
| ENERGY | ★★★★★ |
| DETOX | ★★★☆☆ |
| IMMUNITY | ★★☆☆☆ |
| DIGESTION | ★★★☆☆ |
| SKIN | ★★★☆☆ |

## 132 | orange carrot

4 carrots
1 orange

Double-orange blast of colour and goodness – a great, basic blend
for any morning.

**NUTRIENTS**

Beta-carotene, folic acid, vitamin C;

calcium, magnesium, phosphorus,

potassium, sodium, sulphur

| | |
|---|---|
| ENERGY | ★★★☆☆ |
| DETOX | ★★★☆☆ |
| IMMUNITY | ★★★☆☆ |
| DIGESTION | ★☆☆☆☆ |
| SKIN | ★★☆☆☆ |

## 133 | carrot cleanser

3 carrots
$\frac{1}{2}$ apple
$\frac{1}{2}$ orange
$\frac{1}{4}$ beet (beetroot)
1 stick celery
2 large kale leaves

Any juice using beet or kale can take some getting used to for the vegetable juice
initiate, but once you've had it, you can fully appreciate its cleansing properties.

**NUTRIENTS**

Beta-carotene, folic acid, vitamins B3,

B6 and C; calcium, iron, magnesium,

manganese, phosphorus, potassium,

sodium, sulphur

| | |
|---|---|
| ENERGY | ★★★☆☆ |
| DETOX | ★★★★★ |
| IMMUNITY | ★★★★☆ |
| DIGESTION | ★★★☆☆ |
| SKIN | ★★★☆☆ |

# 134 | carrot deep cleanser

3 carrots
½ apple
½ beet (beetroot)
1 stick celery
3 large kale leaves

If you are at all wary of having beet or kale juice, start with the Carrot Cleanser before you graduate to this one.

**NUTRIENTS**

Beta-carotene, folic acid, vitamins B3, B6 and C; calcium, iron, magnesium, manganese, phosphorus, potassium, sodium, sulphur

| ENERGY | ★★★☆☆ |
| DETOX | ★★★★★ |
| IMMUNITY | ★★★★☆ |
| DIGESTION | ★★★☆☆ |
| SKIN | ★★★☆☆ |

# 135 | carrot crunch

4 carrots
2 sticks celery
½ inch (1 cm) ginger root

Well, of course this isn't crunchy but if it weren't a juice it would certainly get your jaw moving. An excellent contrasting blend of flavours.

**NUTRIENTS**

Beta-carotene, folic acid, vitamin C; calcium, magnesium, phosphorus, potassium, sodium, sulphur

| ENERGY | ★★★☆☆ |
| DETOX | ★★★☆☆ |
| IMMUNITY | ★★★★☆ |
| DIGESTION | ★★★☆☆ |
| SKIN | ★★★☆☆ |

# 136 | carrot digestif

4 carrots
¼ pineapple
2 large white cabbage leaves

The beta-carotene in the carrots, combined with the particularly soothing constituents of the other ingredients, makes this a great juice for helping ease digestive problems.

**NUTRIENTS**

Beta-carotene, folic acid, vitamin C; calcium, magnesium, manganese, phosphorus, potassium, sodium, sulphur

| ENERGY | ★★★☆☆ |
| DETOX | ★★★☆☆ |
| IMMUNITY | ★☆☆☆☆ |
| DIGESTION | ★★★★★ |
| SKIN | ★★★☆☆ |

## 137 | carotene catapult

3 carrots
½ melon
1 slice watermelon
1 teaspoon spirulina

Beta-carotene is a crucial vitamin, which the body can convert to vitamin A.
It's needed for healthy immunity, skin, digestive tract, lungs and much more.
All of the ingredients in this tasty juice are excellent beta-carotene sources.

### NUTRIENTS

Beta-carotene, folic acid, vitamins B1, B3,
B5, B6 and C; calcium, iron, magnesium,
phosphorus, potassium, sodium,
sulphur; protein, essential fatty acids

| | |
|---|---|
| ENERGY | ★★★★☆ |
| DETOX | ★★★☆☆ |
| IMMUNITY | ★★★★★ |
| DIGESTION | ★★★☆☆ |
| SKIN | ★★★★★ |

## 138 | sweet pepper

3 carrots
1 red bell pepper
1 yellow bell pepper

The sweetness of the carrots with bell peppers is remarkable and makes
this fresh drink a great introduction to vegetable-based juicing.

### NUTRIENTS

Beta-carotene, folic acid, vitamin C;
calcium, magnesium, phosphorus,
potassium, sodium, sulphur

| | |
|---|---|
| ENERGY | ★★★☆☆ |
| DETOX | ★★☆☆☆ |
| IMMUNITY | ★★★★★ |
| DIGESTION | ★★☆☆☆ |
| SKIN | ★★★★☆ |

## 139 | breath freshener

4 medium carrots
1 handful parsley

This juice helps work on your breath from the inside, rather than just
washing out your mouth.

### NUTRIENTS

Beta-carotene, folic acid, vitamin B3,
vitamin C; calcium, iron, magnesium,
phosphorus, potassium, sodium, sulphur

| | |
|---|---|
| ENERGY | ★★★★☆ |
| DETOX | ★★★☆☆ |
| IMMUNITY | ★★★★☆ |
| DIGESTION | ★★★★☆ |
| SKIN | ★★★★☆ |

# 140 | veggie carotene catapult

3 carrots
1 red bell pepper
1 spear broccoli
½ sweet potato

Superbly rich in anti-ageing
and cancer-protective carotenes
– and it tastes good.

## NUTRIENTS

Beta-carotene, folic acid, vitamins C,
B5 and E; calcium, magnesium,
phosphorus, potassium, sodium,
sulphur

ENERGY      ★★★★☆
DETOX       ★★★☆☆
IMMUNITY    ★★★★★
DIGESTION   ★★★☆☆
SKIN        ★★★★★

# 141 | cold war

4 carrots
1 orange
½ inch (1 cm) ginger root
2 cloves garlic

The garlic in here is purely for therapeutic use – to give your immune
system a powerful punch in the face of a cold or any other infection.
It's a brave person who can stomach it on any normal morning, let
alone the breath you're likely to have afterwards. If your chest is feeling
congested, you could add half an onion.

## NUTRIENTS

Beta-carotene, folic acid, vitamin C;
calcium, magnesium, phosphorus,
potassium, sodium, sulphur

ENERGY      ★★★☆☆
DETOX       ★★☆☆☆
IMMUNITY    ★★★★★
DIGESTION   ★★☆☆☆
SKIN        ★★★★☆

## 142 | sharp carrot

4 carrots
2 sticks celery
1 lime
1 small bunch fresh mint

This one has a fantastic bite from the lime, nicely lifted by the salty celery and hint of mint.

### NUTRIENTS

Beta-carotene, folic acid, vitamin C;
calcium, magnesium, phosphorus,
potassium, sodium, sulphur

| | |
|---|---|
| ENERGY | ★★★★☆ |
| DETOX | ★★★☆☆ |
| IMMUNITY | ★★★☆☆ |
| DIGESTION | ★★★☆☆ |
| SKIN | ★★★☆☆ |

## 143 | minty carrot

3 carrots
1 apple
1 stick celery
1 small bunch fresh mint

A creamy, orange-coloured juice that could almost be pure fruit, it's so sweet, but the celery gives it a different turn.

### NUTRIENTS

Beta-carotene, folic acid, vitamin C;
calcium, magnesium, manganese,
phosphorus, potassium, sodium,
sulphur

| | |
|---|---|
| ENERGY | ★★★☆☆ |
| DETOX | ★★★☆☆ |
| IMMUNITY | ★★★★☆ |
| DIGESTION | ★★☆☆☆ |
| SKIN | ★★★☆☆ |

## 144 | carrot salad

3 carrots
2 tomatoes
2 sticks celery
$\frac{1}{2}$ lime

A fantastic blend of vegetable juices – makes you wonder why you would ever buy juice in a carton.

### NUTRIENTS

Beta-carotene, biotin, folic acid, vitamin C;
calcium, magnesium, phosphorus, potassium,
sodium, sulphur

| | |
|---|---|
| ENERGY | ★★★☆☆ |
| DETOX | ★★☆☆☆ |
| IMMUNITY | ★★★☆☆ |
| DIGESTION | ★☆☆☆☆ |
| SKIN | ★★★★☆ |

## 145 | carrot lift

4 carrots
2 sticks celery
1 small bunch fresh parsley
$\frac{1}{2}$ lemon

A very refreshing combination – the creamy, sweet carrot offset by
the other ingredients.

### NUTRIENTS

Beta-carotene, folic acid, vitamin B3,
vitamin C; calcium, iron, magnesium,
phosphorus, potassium, sodium, sulphur

| | |
|---|---|
| ENERGY | ★★★★☆ |
| DETOX | ★★★☆☆ |
| IMMUNITY | ★★★☆☆ |
| DIGESTION | ★★★☆☆ |
| SKIN | ★★★☆☆ |

## 146 | bloody carrot

3 carrots
1 beet (beetroot)
2 sticks celery
$\frac{1}{2}$ lime

A doubly rooty combination of sweetness lifted by the celery and
lime – wonderfully cleansing and fortifying.

### NUTRIENTS

Beta-carotene, folic acid, vitamin C;
calcium, magnesium, manganese,
phosphorus, potassium, sodium,
sulphur

| | |
|---|---|
| ENERGY | ★★★☆☆ |
| DETOX | ★★★★☆ |
| IMMUNITY | ★★★★☆ |
| DIGESTION | ★★☆☆☆ |
| SKIN | ★★★★☆ |

## 147 | green hit

3 carrots
2 sticks celery
1 bunch watercress
1 large handful spinach

This is another very cleansing combination with earthy, grassy undertones.

### NUTRIENTS

Beta-carotene, folic acid, vitamins B3,
C and E; calcium, iron, magnesium,
manganese, phosphorus, potassium,
sodium, sulphur

| | |
|---|---|
| ENERGY | ★★☆☆☆ |
| DETOX | ★★★☆☆ |
| IMMUNITY | ★★★☆☆ |
| DIGESTION | ★☆☆☆☆ |
| SKIN | ★★★☆☆ |

## 148 | carrot cooler

3 carrots
½ long cucumber
½ lime

Just the idea of cucumber is refreshing, let alone when you're drinking
the juice, and it contrasts wonderfully well with the carrot.

**NUTRIENTS**

Beta-carotene, folic acid, vitamin C;
calcium, magnesium, phosphorus,
potassium, sodium, sulphur

| | |
|---|---|
| ENERGY | ★★★★☆ |
| DETOX | ★★★☆☆ |
| IMMUNITY | ★★★☆☆ |
| DIGESTION | ★☆☆☆☆ |
| SKIN | ★★★★☆ |

## 149 | florida carrot

3 carrots
½ grapefruit
1 orange
1 small handful mint leaves

The tang of the citrus complements the sweetness of the carrots perfectly.

**NUTRIENTS**

Beta-carotene, folic acid, vitamin C;
calcium, magnesium, phosphorus,
potassium, sodium, sulphur

| | |
|---|---|
| ENERGY | ★★★★☆ |
| DETOX | ★★☆☆☆ |
| IMMUNITY | ★★★★★ |
| DIGESTION | ★☆☆☆☆ |
| SKIN | ★★★☆☆ |

## 150 | chlorophyll carrot

4 carrots
1 orange
1 bunch fresh parsley

A surprisingly good combination and the high chlorophyll content of
the parsley is wonderfully cleansing.

**NUTRIENTS**

Beta-carotene, folic acid, vitamin B3,
vitamin C; calcium, iron, magnesium,
phosphorus, potassium, sodium, sulphur

| | |
|---|---|
| ENERGY | ★★★★☆ |
| DETOX | ★★★★☆ |
| IMMUNITY | ★★★★☆ |
| DIGESTION | ★☆☆☆☆ |
| SKIN | ★★★★☆ |

# 151 | carrot tang

3 carrots
1 grapefruit
½ inch (1 cm) ginger root

I love the tang of the grapefruit tempered by the creamy carrot and then lifted by the zing of ginger – altogether an uplifting combination.

**NUTRIENTS**

Beta-carotene, folic acid, vitamin C; calcium, magnesium, phosphorus, potassium, sodium, sulphur

| | |
|---|---|
| ENERGY | ★★★★☆ |
| DETOX | ★★☆☆☆ |
| IMMUNITY | ★★★★☆ |
| DIGESTION | ★☆☆☆☆ |
| SKIN | ★★★☆☆ |

# 152 | triple orange

3 carrots
1 orange
½ melon

If you get the orange-fleshed variety of melon you get a threesome of orange and an explosion of tastes and a powerful beta-carotene hit.

**NUTRIENTS**

Beta-carotene, folic acid, vitamin C; calcium, magnesium, phosphorus, potassium, sodium, sulphur

| | |
|---|---|
| ENERGY | ★★★★★ |
| DETOX | ★★☆☆☆ |
| IMMUNITY | ★★★★★ |
| DIGESTION | ★☆☆☆☆ |
| SKIN | ★★★★☆ |

# 153 | capple zing

4 carrots
1 apple
½ inch (1 cm) ginger root
½ lime

Uplifting and fresh on the palate. This is a wonderful morning combination – very refreshing to awaken your tastebuds for the day.

**NUTRIENTS**

Beta-carotene, folic acid, vitamin C; calcium, magnesium, phosphorus, potassium, sodium, sulphur

| | |
|---|---|
| ENERGY | ★★★☆☆ |
| DETOX | ★★☆☆☆ |
| IMMUNITY | ★★★☆☆ |
| DIGESTION | ★☆☆☆☆ |
| SKIN | ★★☆☆☆ |

## 154 | capple kiwi

3 carrots
1 apple
2 kiwis

Kiwis can often be a bit soft to juice – choose firm ones and you'll get a delicious green juice. A crisp apple such as Discovery goes particularly well here.

**NUTRIENTS**

Beta-carotene, folic acid, vitamin C;
calcium, magnesium, phosphorus,
potassium, sodium, sulphur

| | |
|---|---|
| ENERGY | ★★★★★ |
| DETOX | ★★★☆☆ |
| IMMUNITY | ★★★★☆ |
| DIGESTION | ★★☆☆☆ |
| SKIN | ★★★★☆ |

## 155 | capple and black

4 carrots
1 apple
1 handful blackcurrants

That traditional favourite of apple and blackcurrant mixed with creamy, sweet carrots makes a great combination.

**NUTRIENTS**

Beta-carotene, biotin, folic acid,
vitamin C, vitamin E; calcium,
magnesium, manganese, phosphorus,
potassium, sodium, sulphur

| | |
|---|---|
| ENERGY | ★★★☆☆ |
| DETOX | ★★☆☆☆ |
| IMMUNITY | ★★★★☆ |
| DIGESTION | ★☆☆☆☆ |
| SKIN | ★★★☆☆ |

## 156 | carrot jointaid

3 carrots
$\frac{1}{2}$ pineapple
1 inch (2.5 cm) ginger root
1 tablespoon (15 ml) flaxseed (linseed) oil

A great combination of antioxidants and essential fats to help soothe joints, plus pineapple and ginger which have been shown to be anti-inflammatory and are good for problems such as asthma.

**NUTRIENTS**

Beta-carotene, folic acid, vitamin C;
calcium, magnesium, manganese,
phosphorus, potassium, sodium,
sulphur; essential fatty acids

| | |
|---|---|
| ENERGY | ★★★☆☆ |
| DETOX | ★★★☆☆ |
| IMMUNITY | ★★★☆☆ |
| DIGESTION | ★★★☆☆ |
| SKIN | ★★☆☆☆ |

# 157 | cool 'n' creamy

1 cucumber
4 carrots

Each of these juices brings out the best in the other. You'll be surprised at just how much flavour you can extract from juicing a cucumber, and how delicious it is.

**NUTRIENTS**

Beta-carotene, folic acid, vitamin C;
calcium, magnesium, phosphorus,
potassium, sodium, sulphur

| | |
|---|---|
| ENERGY | ★★☆☆☆ |
| DETOX | ★★★☆☆ |
| IMMUNITY | ★★☆☆☆ |
| DIGESTION | ★☆☆☆☆ |
| SKIN | ★★☆☆☆ |

# 158 | cool 'n' pale

1 cucumber
2 apples

A dreamy shade of green, with a taste to match — this refreshing combination of two highly juicy ingredients is very cleansing on the palate.

**NUTRIENTS**

Beta-carotene, folic acid,
vitamin C; calcium, magnesium,
phosphorus, potassium, sulphur

| | |
|---|---|
| ENERGY | ★★★☆☆ |
| DETOX | ★★★★☆ |
| IMMUNITY | ★★☆☆☆ |
| DIGESTION | ★★★☆☆ |
| SKIN | ★★★☆☆ |

## 159 | cucumber refresher

1 cucumber
2 pears

Another delicate mix of pale green with two subtly flavoured ingredients blending to form a refreshing, cleansing juice.

### NUTRIENTS

Beta-carotene, folic acid, vitamin C; calcium, magnesium, phosphorus, potassium, sulphur

| | |
|---|---|
| ENERGY | ★★★☆☆ |
| DETOX | ★★★★☆ |
| IMMUNITY | ★★☆☆☆ |
| DIGESTION | ★★★☆☆ |
| SKIN | ★★★☆☆ |

## 160 | apple cooler

1 cucumber
2 apples
4 sprigs fresh mint
$\frac{1}{2}$ inch (1 cm) ginger root

A wonderful summer drink. You could even add a splash of ginger ale or fizzy water for a non-alcoholic cocktail.

### NUTRIENTS

Beta-carotene, folic acid, vitamin C; calcium, magnesium, phosphorus, potassium, sulphur

| | |
|---|---|
| ENERGY | ★★★☆☆ |
| DETOX | ★★★★☆ |
| IMMUNITY | ★★☆☆☆ |
| DIGESTION | ★★★☆☆ |
| SKIN | ★★★☆☆ |

## 161 | mellow melon

$\frac{3}{4}$ cucumber
$\frac{1}{2}$ melon
1 pear
2 sprigs mint

From the same family, cucumber and melon combine beautifully. You can leave out the mint if you prefer.

### NUTRIENTS

Beta-carotene, folic acid, vitamin C; calcium, magnesium, phosphorus, potassium, sodium, sulphur

| | |
|---|---|
| ENERGY | ★★★★☆ |
| DETOX | ★★★★☆ |
| IMMUNITY | ★★★☆☆ |
| DIGESTION | ★★★☆☆ |
| SKIN | ★★★☆☆ |

# 162 | water water everywhere

1 cucumber
1 thick slice watermelon

Two of the juiciest of nature's pickings blend to create a rich but subtle flavour. A perfect summer thirst-quencher.

**NUTRIENTS**

Beta-carotene, folic acid, vitamin B5, vitamin C; calcium, magnesium, phosphorus, potassium, sodium

| | |
|---|---|
| ENERGY | ★★★★☆ |
| DETOX | ★★★★☆ |
| IMMUNITY | ★★★★☆ |
| DIGESTION | ★★☆☆☆ |
| SKIN | ★★★☆☆ |

# 163 | citrus cuke

1 cucumber
1 orange
1 grapefruit

Although the actual flavour of the cucumber gets a bit lost, its watery freshness transforms the orange and grapefruit to a more refreshing drink.

**NUTRIENTS**

Beta-carotene, folic acid, vitamin C; calcium, magnesium, phosphorus, potassium, sulphur

| | |
|---|---|
| ENERGY | ★★★★☆ |
| DETOX | ★★☆☆☆ |
| IMMUNITY | ★★★★☆ |
| DIGESTION | ☆☆☆☆☆ |
| SKIN | ★★★☆☆ |

# 164 | salad cooler

1 cucumber
3 tomatoes
1 small bunch fresh parsley
$\frac{1}{2}$ lemon

A great veggie cocktail which always reminds me of a fresh, tasty Middle Eastern salad.

**NUTRIENTS**

Beta-carotene, biotin, folic acid, vitamin B3, vitamin C; calcium, iron, magnesium, phosphorus, potassium, sodium, sulphur

| | |
|---|---|
| ENERGY | ★★☆☆☆ |
| DETOX | ★★★★☆ |
| IMMUNITY | ★★★☆☆ |
| DIGESTION | ★☆☆☆☆ |
| SKIN | ★★★★☆ |

# 165 | tropical cucumber

1 cucumber
2 guavas
1 apple

The rich, tangy, tropical taste of guavas
is toned down by the cucumber to form
an unusual cooling juice.

**NUTRIENTS**

Beta-carotene, folic acid, vitamin B3,
vitamin C; calcium, magnesium, phosphorus,
potassium, sodium, sulphur

| | |
|---|---|
| ENERGY | ★★★★☆ |
| DETOX | ★★★★☆ |
| IMMUNITY | ★★★★☆ |
| DIGESTION | ★★☆☆☆ |
| SKIN | ★★★★☆ |

# 166 | bloody cuke

1 cucumber
2 apples
1 beet (beetroot)

The richness of the beet is perfectly tempered by the cucumber
and sweetened by the apple in this colourful magenta juice.

**NUTRIENTS**

Beta-carotene, folic acid, vitamin C;
calcium, magnesium, phosphorus,
potassium, sodium, sulphur

| | |
|---|---|
| ENERGY | ★★★☆☆ |
| DETOX | ★★★★★ |
| IMMUNITY | ★★★☆☆ |
| DIGESTION | ★★★★☆ |
| SKIN | ★★★★☆ |

# 167 | green goddess

1 bunch fresh parsley
1 handful watercress
4 broccoli spears
½ pineapple

There had to be one juice with this name and this is it – anything with pineapple is good in my book.

## NUTRIENTS

Beta-carotene, folic acid, vitamins B3, B5, C and E; calcium, iron, magnesium, phosphorus, potassium, sodium, sulphur

| | |
|---|---|
| ENERGY | ★★★☆☆ |
| DETOX | ★★★★★ |
| IMMUNITY | ★★☆☆☆ |
| DIGESTION | ★★★★☆ |
| SKIN | ★★★★☆ |

# 168 | green apple

8 spears broccoli
1 bunch parsley
3 apples

To counteract the strong-tasting green vegetables, it's best to use an apple variety with a strong flavour, such as Granny Smith, for this one.

## NUTRIENTS

Beta-carotene, folic acid, vitamins B3, B5 and C; calcium, iron, magnesium, phosphorus, potassium, sodium, sulphur

| | |
|---|---|
| ENERGY | ★★☆☆☆ |
| DETOX | ★★★★★ |
| IMMUNITY | ★★★★☆ |
| DIGESTION | ★★★★☆ |
| SKIN | ★★★★☆ |

# 169 | green 'n' pear it

8 spears broccoli
3 sticks celery
2 pears

You may not wish to adulterate your pear with broccoli juice but believe me, it's a surprising winner.

## NUTRIENTS

Beta-carotene, folic acid, vitamin B5, vitamin C; calcium, magnesium, phosphorus, potassium, sodium, sulphur

| | |
|---|---|
| ENERGY | ★★★☆☆ |
| DETOX | ★★★★★ |
| IMMUNITY | ★★★★☆ |
| DIGESTION | ★★★★☆ |
| SKIN | ★★★★☆ |

## 170 | green citrus

2 handfuls spinach
2 sticks celery
2 oranges

The orange juice is so flavourful that it can carry pretty much anything, even the powerful taste of iron-rich spinach.

**NUTRIENTS**

Beta-carotene, folic acid, vitamin B3, vitamin C; calcium, iron, magnesium, phosphorus, potassium, sodium, sulphur

| | |
|---|---|
| ENERGY | ★★★☆☆ |
| DETOX | ★★★☆☆ |
| IMMUNITY | ★★★★☆ |
| DIGESTION | ★☆☆☆☆ |
| SKIN | ★★★☆☆ |

## 171 | green grapefruit

8 broccoli spears
2 grapefruits

If anything is going to temper the strong, earthy taste of broccoli juice and make it more palatable, it's going to be grapefruit.

**NUTRIENTS**

Beta-carotene, folic acid, vitamin B5, vitamin C; calcium, magnesium, phosphorus, potassium, sodium, sulphur

| | |
|---|---|
| ENERGY | ★★★☆☆ |
| DETOX | ★★★★★ |
| IMMUNITY | ★★★★☆ |
| DIGESTION | ★☆☆☆☆ |
| SKIN | ★★★★☆ |

## 172 | green waldorf

5 large kale leaves
2 apples
2 sticks celery
1 tablespoon (15 ml) flaxseed (linseed) oil

Well, not quite a Waldorf, but it tastes good and is super-healthy. The flax brings an unusual dimension in taste, texture and health properties to this cleansing juice.

**NUTRIENTS**

Beta-carotene, folic acid, vitamin B3, vitamin C; calcium, iron, magnesium, manganese, phosphorus, potassium, sodium, sulphur

| | |
|---|---|
| ENERGY | ★★★☆☆ |
| DETOX | ★★★★☆ |
| IMMUNITY | ★★★☆☆ |
| DIGESTION | ★★★★☆ |
| SKIN | ★★★★☆ |

## 173 | sweet green melon

1 bunch parsley
$\frac{1}{4}$ white cabbage
$\frac{1}{2}$ long cucumber
$\frac{1}{2}$ melon

The green in this doesn't just belong to the melon – it's a cleansing punch, tempered by cucumber.

### NUTRIENTS

Beta-carotene, folic acid, vitamins B3,
C and E; calcium, iron, magnesium,
phosphorus, potassium, sodium,
sulphur

| | |
|---|---|
| ENERGY | ★★★☆☆ |
| DETOX | ★★★★☆ |
| IMMUNITY | ★★★☆☆ |
| DIGESTION | ★★★★★ |
| SKIN | ★★★★☆ |

## 174 | green lullaby

$\frac{1}{2}$ lettuce
2 apples
$\frac{1}{2}$ lime
1 small handful spinach

Lettuces contain substances which act as mild sedatives, so this one should help send you into the land of nod.

### NUTRIENTS

Beta-carotene, folic acid, vitamin B3,
vitamin C; calcium, iron, magnesium,
phosphorus, potassium, sodium, sulphur

| | |
|---|---|
| ENERGY | ★☆☆☆☆ |
| DETOX | ★★★☆☆ |
| IMMUNITY | ★★★☆☆ |
| DIGESTION | ☆☆☆☆☆ |
| SKIN | ★★☆☆☆ |

## 175 | super defender

5 large kale leaves
3 carrots
1 orange

Kale, orange and carrot – muddy to look at, magnificent to taste.

### NUTRIENTS

Beta-carotene, folic acid, vitamin B3,
vitamin C; calcium, iron, magnesium,
manganese, phosphorus, potassium,
sodium, sulphur

| | |
|---|---|
| ENERGY | ★★★☆☆ |
| DETOX | ★★★★☆ |
| IMMUNITY | ★★★★★ |
| DIGESTION | ☆☆☆☆☆ |
| SKIN | ★★★★☆ |

## 176 | grape & green

4 large kale leaves
2 handfuls spinach
2 sticks celery
1 grapefruit

The tangy grapefruit and salty celery cut right through the earthy taste of the greens in this rejuvenating juice.

### NUTRIENTS

Beta-carotene, folic acid, vitamin C; calcium, magnesium, manganese, phosphorus, potassium, sodium, sulphur

| | |
|---|---|
| ENERGY | ★★☆☆☆ |
| DETOX | ★★★★☆ |
| IMMUNITY | ★★★★☆ |
| DIGESTION | ★★☆☆☆ |
| SKIN | ★★★★☆ |

## 177 | creamy green

1 bunch parsley
1 handful watercress
4 carrots
1 lime

The sweet, creamy carrot juice carries the greens very well, and the lime gives it a good, sharp kick.

### NUTRIENTS

Beta-carotene, folic acid, vitamins B3, C and E; calcium, iron, magnesium, phosphorus, potassium, sodium, sulphur

| | |
|---|---|
| ENERGY | ★★★☆☆ |
| DETOX | ★★★★★ |
| IMMUNITY | ★★★★★ |
| DIGESTION | ★★★☆☆ |
| SKIN | ★★★★☆ |

## 178 | red & green

1 bunch parsley
1 lemon
5 tomatoes

This is a fantastically cleansing juice, and another one with Middle Eastern salad undertones.

### NUTRIENTS

Beta-carotene, biotin, folic acid, vitamin B3, vitamin C; calcium, iron, magnesium, phosphorus, potassium, sodium, sulphur

| | |
|---|---|
| ENERGY | ★★★☆☆ |
| DETOX | ★★★★☆ |
| IMMUNITY | ★★★★☆ |
| DIGESTION | ★☆☆☆☆ |
| SKIN | ★★★★☆ |

# 179 | beet basic

2 beets (beetroot)
2 carrots
1 apple
1 orange
1 sticks celery
$\frac{1}{2}$ inch (1 cm) ginger root

If I have beets in the refrigerator, this is one of my standard morning
juices. It's a supreme energy-lifting, cleansing and immune-boosting blend.

**NUTRIENTS**

Beta-carotene, folic acid, vitamin C;
calcium, magnesium, phosphorus,
potassium, sodium, sulphur

| | |
|---|---|
| ENERGY | ★★★★☆ |
| DETOX | ★★★★☆ |
| IMMUNITY | ★★★★☆ |
| DIGESTION | ★★★☆☆ |
| SKIN | ★★★★☆ |

# 180 | beetles

2 beets (beetroot)
2 apples
3 sticks celery

Another great combination
of beet and fruit, enhanced
by the celery.

**NUTRIENTS**

Beta-carotene, folic acid, vitamin C;
calcium, magnesium, phosphorus,
potassium, sodium, sulphur

| | |
|---|---|
| ENERGY | ★★★★☆ |
| DETOX | ★★★★★ |
| IMMUNITY | ★★★☆☆ |
| DIGESTION | ★★★☆☆ |
| SKIN | ★★★★☆ |

## 181 | blood 'n' grape

2 beets (beetroot)
1 grapefruit
2 sticks celery

Grapefruit carries that earthy, sweet beet well and both are lifted by
the salty celery – a convincing introduction to beet, if you need one.

### NUTRIENTS

Beta-carotene, folic acid, vitamin C;
calcium, magnesium, phosphorus,
potassium, sodium, sulphur

| | |
|---|---|
| ENERGY | ★★★★☆ |
| DETOX | ★★★★☆ |
| IMMUNITY | ★★★★☆ |
| DIGESTION | ★★☆☆☆ |
| SKIN | ★★★★☆ |

## 182 | blood & carrots

2 beets (beetroot)
2 oranges (ideally blood oranges)
4 carrots

Blood oranges or not, this sumptuous juice is going to be a rich,
purple colour, swirling with the creamy orange from the carrots.

### NUTRIENTS

Beta-carotene, folic acid, vitamin C;
calcium, magnesium, phosphorus,
potassium, sodium, sulphur

| | |
|---|---|
| ENERGY | ★★★★☆ |
| DETOX | ★★★☆☆ |
| IMMUNITY | ★★★★★ |
| DIGESTION | ★★☆☆☆ |
| SKIN | ★★★★☆ |

## 183 | rooty pear

3 parsnips
3 pears
1 lime

A blend of very delicate, sweet flavours, sharpened by the lime.

### NUTRIENTS

Beta-carotene, folic acid, vitamin C;
calcium, magnesium, phosphorus,
potassium, sodium, sulphur

| | |
|---|---|
| ENERGY | ★★★★☆ |
| DETOX | ★★☆☆☆ |
| IMMUNITY | ★★★☆☆ |
| DIGESTION | ★☆☆☆☆ |
| SKIN | ★★☆☆☆ |

## 184 | apples & neeps

3 parsnips
3 apples
½ lime
3 sprigs mint

If you're at all hesitant to try root vegetable juice, this is a good one
to start with. Add more lime if you want to give it more tang.

**NUTRIENTS**

Beta-carotene, folic acid, vitamin C;
calcium, magnesium, phosphorus,
potassium, sodium, sulphur

| | |
|---|---|
| ENERGY | ★★★★☆ |
| DETOX | ★★★☆☆ |
| IMMUNITY | ★★★☆☆ |
| DIGESTION | ★★☆☆☆ |
| SKIN | ★★☆☆☆ |

## 185 | carotene kick

1 sweet potato
½ melon
3 carrots

Sweet potatoes are a delicious, rich source of carotene, as are the other
ingredients in this vibrant orange drink.

**NUTRIENTS**

Beta-carotene, folic acid, vitamin C,
vitamin E; calcium, magnesium, phosphorus,
potassium, sodium, sulphur

| | |
|---|---|
| ENERGY | ★★★★★ |
| DETOX | ★★★☆☆ |
| IMMUNITY | ★★★★★ |
| DIGESTION | ★★★☆☆ |
| SKIN | ★★★★★ |

## 186 | pineroot

1 sweet potato
1 carrot
½ pineapple

The root vegetables tone down the tangy pineapple for a sweet drink.

**NUTRIENTS**

Beta-carotene, folic acid, vitamin C,
vitamin E; calcium, magnesium, manganese,
phosphorus, potassium, sodium, sulphur

| | |
|---|---|
| ENERGY | ★★★★★ |
| DETOX | ★★★☆☆ |
| IMMUNITY | ★★★★★ |
| DIGESTION | ★★★★★ |
| SKIN | ★★★★☆ |

## 187 | pure tomato

8 tomatoes
salt, pepper, Tobasco,
Worcestershire Sauce to taste

One of the few vegetable juices that is wonderful unadulterated. You can
always add a squeeze of lemon juice if you're not into the pure stuff.

**NUTRIENTS**

| | | |
|---|---|---|
| Beta-carotene, biotin, folic acid, | ENERGY | ★★★★☆ |
| vitamin C; calcium, magnesium, | DETOX | ★★☆☆☆ |
| phosphorus, potassium, sodium, | IMMUNITY | ★★★★☆ |
| sulphur | DIGESTION | ☆☆☆☆☆ |
| | SKIN | ★★★★☆ |

## 188 | ginger tom

6 tomatoes
2 sticks celery
1 inch (2.5 cm) ginger root

Celery is probably my favourite juice to combine with tomatoes – the
light saltiness taking the edge off the richer tomato and the ginger in
this one gives it all a sharp lift. You can be even more daring with the
amount of ginger you use if you like.

**NUTRIENTS**

| | | |
|---|---|---|
| Beta-carotene, biotin, folic acid, | ENERGY | ★★★★☆ |
| vitamin C; calcium, magnesium, | DETOX | ★★☆☆☆ |
| manganese, phosphorus, potassium, | IMMUNITY | ★★★★☆ |
| sodium, sulphur | DIGESTION | ★☆☆☆☆ |
| | SKIN | ★★★★☆ |

## 189 | tabouleh

6 tomatoes
1 large bunch parsley
1 lemon
salt and pepper to taste

If you are a fan of tomato and parsley salad or tabouleh, you'll love this
one. Season with some salt and pepper.

**NUTRIENTS**

| | | |
|---|---|---|
| Beta-carotene, biotin, folic acid, | ENERGY | ★★★☆☆ |
| vitamin B3, vitamin C; calcium, iron, | DETOX | ★★★☆☆ |
| magnesium, phosphorus, potassium, | IMMUNITY | ★★★★☆ |
| sodium, sulphur | DIGESTION | ★☆☆☆☆ |
| | SKIN | ★★★★☆ |

# 190 | tomato bell

6 tomatoes
2 bell peppers
1 stick celery
$\frac{1}{2}$ lemon
salt, pepper, Tobasco,
Worcestershire Sauce to taste

I'd only use red or yellow peppers for this as
the green ones tend to take over the other
flavours. Season it well once you've made
the juice, sit back and sip it slowly, nibbling
from a bowl of potato chips, nuts and olives.

## NUTRIENTS
Beta-carotene, biotin, folic acid, vitamin B3,
vitamin C; calcium, iron, magnesium,
phosphorus, potassium, sodium, sulphur

| | |
|---|---|
| ENERGY | ★★★★☆ |
| DETOX | ★★☆☆☆ |
| IMMUNITY | ★★★★☆ |
| DIGESTION | ☆☆☆☆☆ |
| SKIN | ★★★☆☆ |

# 191 | peppery tom

6 tomatoes
1 large bunch watercress
1 stick celery

The watercress in this acts as a seasoning all to itself, and the celery
lightens the rich taste of the tomatoes.

## NUTRIENTS
Beta-carotene, biotin, folic acid,
vitamin C, vitamin E; calcium,
iron, magnesium, phosphorus,
potassium, sodium, sulphur

| | |
|---|---|
| ENERGY | ★★★★☆ |
| DETOX | ★★★★☆ |
| IMMUNITY | ★★★★☆ |
| DIGESTION | ★☆☆☆☆ |
| SKIN | ★★★★☆ |

## 192 | sweet 'n' fresh

6 tomatoes
1 red bell pepper
1 stick celery
1 large bunch parsley

The wonderful sweetness of the tomatoes and peppers is heightened by the salty celery and freshened further by the parsley.

### NUTRIENTS

Beta-carotene, biotin, folic acid,
vitamin B3, vitamin C; calcium, iron,
magnesium, manganese, phosphorus,
potassium, sodium, sulphur

| | |
|---|---|
| ENERGY | ★★★★☆ |
| DETOX | ★★★☆☆ |
| IMMUNITY | ★★★★☆ |
| DIGESTION | ★☆☆☆☆ |
| SKIN | ★★★★☆ |

## 193 | classic combo

6 tomatoes
3 carrots
1 lime
1 small bunch mint

The two most popular and palatable of the vegetable juices combined with a lift from the mint and lime.

### NUTRIENTS

Beta-carotene, biotin, folic acid,
vitamin C; calcium, magnesium,
phosphorus, potassium, sodium,
sulphur

| | |
|---|---|
| ENERGY | ★★★★☆ |
| DETOX | ★★★☆☆ |
| IMMUNITY | ★★★★☆ |
| DIGESTION | ★☆☆☆☆ |
| SKIN | ★★★★☆ |

## 194 | green tomatoes

4 tomatoes
½ long cucumber
1 large handful spinach leaves
4 broccoli spears

Not fried like at the Whistlestop Café, but blended with greens for a deep cleansing juice. The earthy, green taste of the spinach and broccoli is nicely hidden by the other ingredients.

### NUTRIENTS

Beta-carotene, biotin, folic acid,
vitamin B3, vitamin C; calcium, iron,
magnesium, phosphorus, potassium,
sodium, sulphur

| | |
|---|---|
| ENERGY | ★★★☆☆ |
| DETOX | ★★★★☆ |
| IMMUNITY | ★★★☆☆ |
| DIGESTION | ☆☆☆☆☆ |
| SKIN | ★★☆☆☆ |

## 195 | root tomato

4 tomatoes
4 carrots
1 handful radishes
salt, pepper and a squeeze of lemon to taste

No, not a tomato modified to grow underground, but a blend with
wonderfully contrasting vegetables that do.

**NUTRIENTS**

Beta-carotene, biotin, folic acid,
vitamin C; calcium, magnesium,
phosphorus, potassium, sodium,
sulphur

| | |
|---|---|
| ENERGY | ★★★★☆ |
| DETOX | ★★☆☆☆ |
| IMMUNITY | ★★★★☆ |
| DIGESTION | ★☆☆☆☆ |
| SKIN | ★★★★☆ |

## 196 | tricolore

6 tomatoes
2 parsnips
2 sticks celery
1 small handful of basil leaves

No mozzarella in here, but a red, white and green combination
anyway, and the unusual touch from the basil will transport you
straight to Italy.

**NUTRIENTS**

Beta-carotene, biotin, folic acid,
vitamin C; calcium, magnesium,
manganese, phosphorus, potassium,
sodium, sulphur

| | |
|---|---|
| ENERGY | ★★★★☆ |
| DETOX | ★★★☆☆ |
| IMMUNITY | ★★★☆☆ |
| DIGESTION | ★☆☆☆☆ |
| SKIN | ★★★☆☆ |

## 197 | red tomato

6 tomatoes
1 beet (beetroot)
1 lemon

You may have found by now that unlike tomato juice from a carton,
the stuff you make at home is not red but pink, so the title may not
be stating the obvious. Here it's the inimitable velvet red-purple of
the beet that colours the juice.

**NUTRIENTS**

Beta-carotene, biotin, folic acid,
vitamin C; calcium, magnesium,
phosphorus, potassium, sodium,
sulphur

| | |
|---|---|
| ENERGY | ★★★★☆ |
| DETOX | ★★★★☆ |
| IMMUNITY | ★★★★★ |
| DIGESTION | ☆☆☆☆☆ |
| SKIN | ★★★☆☆ |

## 198 | black mud

5 tomatoes
1 beet (beetroot)
4 large kale leaves
1 lime

Not the most appetizing colour but it sure makes up for that in taste
and some unbeatable health benefits.

### NUTRIENTS

Beta-carotene, biotin, folic acid,
vitamin B3, vitamin C; calcium, iron,
magnesium, manganese, phosphorus,
potassium, sodium, sulphur

| | |
|---|---|
| ENERGY | ★★★★☆ |
| DETOX | ★★★★★ |
| IMMUNITY | ★★★★★ |
| DIGESTION | ★☆☆☆☆ |
| SKIN | ★★★☆☆ |

## 199 | cool as a tomato

5 tomatoes
½ long cucumber
salt, pepper, Tobasco, Worcestershire Sauce to taste

As always with juices containing cucumber, this is a light, refreshing
blend and another one which goes down well with some seasoning.

### NUTRIENTS

Beta-carotene, biotin, folic acid,
vitamin C; calcium, magnesium,
phosphorus, potassium, sodium,
sulphur

| | |
|---|---|
| ENERGY | ★★★☆☆ |
| DETOX | ★★☆☆☆ |
| IMMUNITY | ★★★☆☆ |
| DIGESTION | ☆☆☆☆☆ |
| SKIN | ★★☆☆☆ |

## 200 | tomato cocktail

6 tomatoes
¼ long cucumber
½ inch (1 cm) ginger root
1 small bunch mint leaves
1 lime

The cucumber is added to refresh, and then the mint, lime and ginger
to take it all onto an even higher plane.

### NUTRIENTS

Beta-carotene, biotin, folic acid,
vitamin C; calcium, magnesium,
phosphorus, potassium, sodium,
sulphur

| | |
|---|---|
| ENERGY | ★★★☆☆ |
| DETOX | ★★☆☆☆ |
| IMMUNITY | ★★★☆☆ |
| DIGESTION | ★☆☆☆☆ |
| SKIN | ★★☆☆☆ |

# 201 | classic & green

6 tomatoes
3 carrots
1 large handful spinach

Classic with an earthy, green undertone,
this juice is particularly good for the
immune system as it's packed with carotenes.

**NUTRIENTS**

Beta-carotene, biotin, folic acid,
vitamin B3, vitamin C; calcium,
iron, magnesium, phosphorus,
potassium, sodium, sulphur

ENERGY ★★★★☆
DETOX ★★★☆☆
IMMUNITY ★★★★★
DIGESTION ☆☆☆☆☆
SKIN ★★★★☆

# 202 | old favourites

4 tomatoes
1 orange
2 carrots

Three of the most popular individual juices rolled into one to create
an interesting tasting juice that is great for your immunity.

**NUTRIENTS**

Beta-carotene, biotin, folic acid,
vitamin C; calcium, magnesium,
phosphorus, potassium, sodium,
sulphur

ENERGY ★★★★☆
DETOX ★★☆☆☆
IMMUNITY ★★★★★
DIGESTION ☆☆☆☆☆
SKIN ★★★★☆

## 203 | tomorange

4 tomatoes
2 oranges

Probably the only combination of tomato juice with fruit that
I think really works – very refreshing and very good for you.

**NUTRIENTS**

Beta-carotene, biotin, folic acid,
vitamin C; calcium, magnesium,
phosphorus, potassium, sodium,
sulphur

| | |
|---|---|
| ENERGY | ★★★★☆ |
| DETOX | ★★☆☆☆ |
| IMMUNITY | ★★★★★ |
| DIGESTION | ☆☆☆☆☆ |
| SKIN | ★★★☆☆ |

## 204 | tomorange fresh

4 tomatoes
2 oranges
1 small handful fresh mint leaves

Just as above with a hint of mint that takes it up a notch in the
refreshing stakes. A great immune-booster as well.

**NUTRIENTS**

Beta-carotene, biotin, folic acid,
vitamin C; calcium, magnesium,
phosphorus, potassium, sodium,
sulphur

| | |
|---|---|
| ENERGY | ★★★★☆ |
| DETOX | ★★☆☆☆ |
| IMMUNITY | ★★★★★ |
| DIGESTION | ★☆☆☆☆ |
| SKIN | ★★★☆☆ |

# 205 | creamy crunch

4 sticks celery
3 carrots

Each of these juices brings out the best in the other.

**NUTRIENTS**

Beta-carotene, folic acid, vitamin C;
calcium, magnesium, manganese,
phosphorus, potassium, sodium,
sulphur

| | |
|---|---|
| ENERGY | ★★★☆☆ |
| DETOX | ★★★★☆ |
| IMMUNITY | ★★★☆☆ |
| DIGESTION | ★★★☆☆ |
| SKIN | ★★★☆☆ |

# 206 | cool 'n' pale II

4 sticks celery
2 apples

A dreamy shade of green, with a taste to match. Discovery apples
make an ideal partner for the celery in this one.

**NUTRIENTS**

Beta-carotene, folic acid, vitamin C;
calcium, magnesium, manganese,
phosphorus, potassium, sodium,
sulphur

| | |
|---|---|
| ENERGY | ★★☆☆☆ |
| DETOX | ★★★☆☆ |
| IMMUNITY | ★★☆☆☆ |
| DIGESTION | ★★★☆☆ |
| SKIN | ★★☆☆☆ |

# 207 | savoury fruit

3 sticks celery
1 apple
1 orange

The celery here lifts the flavours of the fruit juices.

**NUTRIENTS**

Beta-carotene, folic acid, vitamin C;
calcium, magnesium, manganese,
phosphorus, potassium, sodium,
sulphur

| | |
|---|---|
| ENERGY | ★★★☆☆ |
| DETOX | ★★★☆☆ |
| IMMUNITY | ★★★☆☆ |
| DIGESTION | ★☆☆☆☆ |
| SKIN | ★★☆☆☆ |

## 208 | delicate pale

4 sticks celery
2 pears

Because pears tend to have a more delicate
flavour than apples, this one is even more
subtle than Cool 'n' Pale II (see p.105), but is
just as refreshing.

**NUTRIENTS**

Beta-carotene, folic acid, vitamin C;
calcium, magnesium, phosphorus,
potassium, sodium, sulphur

| | |
|---|---|
| ENERGY | ★★★☆☆ |
| DETOX | ★★★★☆ |
| IMMUNITY | ★★☆☆☆ |
| DIGESTION | ★★★☆☆ |
| SKIN | ★★☆☆☆ |

## 209 | crunch morning favourite

3 sticks celery
1 grapefruit
$\frac{1}{2}$ inch (1 cm) ginger root

One of a few standard morning favourites to come out of my fruit bowl
and refrigerator. Grapefruit always seems to go well with vegetable juices.

**NUTRIENTS**

Beta-carotene, folic acid, vitamin C;
calcium, magnesium, manganese,
phosphorus, potassium, sodium,
sulphur

| | |
|---|---|
| ENERGY | ★★☆☆☆ |
| DETOX | ★★★☆☆ |
| IMMUNITY | ★★★☆☆ |
| DIGESTION | ★☆☆☆☆ |
| SKIN | ★★☆☆☆ |

# 210 | pink punch

3 sticks celery
2 apples
1 handful cranberries (or raspberries)
3 sprigs fresh mint
$\frac{1}{2}$ inch (1 cm) ginger root

Who needs alcohol on
a hot summer's day?

**NUTRIENTS**
Beta-carotene, folic acid,
vitamin C; calcium, iron,
magnesium, manganese,
phosphorus, potassium,
sodium, sulphur

| | |
|---|---|
| ENERGY | ★★★★☆ |
| DETOX | ★★★☆☆ |
| IMMUNITY | ★★★★☆ |
| DIGESTION | ★★☆☆☆ |
| SKIN | ★★☆☆☆ |

# 211 | celery jointaid

3 sticks celery
$\frac{1}{2}$ pineapple
1 inch (2.5 cm) ginger root
1 tablespoon (15 ml) flaxseed (linseed) oil

A combination of minerals, antioxidants and essential fats to help
support healthy joints, this fresh juice also offers the anti-inflammatory
properties of pineapple and ginger.

**NUTRIENTS**
Beta-carotene, folic acid, vitamin C;
calcium, magnesium, manganese,
phosphorus, potassium, sodium,
sulphur; essential fatty acids

| | |
|---|---|
| ENERGY | ★★★★☆ |
| DETOX | ★★★★☆ |
| IMMUNITY | ★★★★★ |
| DIGESTION | ★★★★★ |
| SKIN | ★★★☆☆ |

# 212 | fresh crunch

4 sticks celery
1 apple
5 sprigs fresh mint
1 lime

A startling, fresh combination – use more lime if you fancy giving it a sharper bite.

**NUTRIENTS**

Beta-carotene, folic acid, vitamin C;
calcium, magnesium, manganese,
phosphorus, potassium, sodium,
sulphur

| | |
|---|---|
| ENERGY | ★★☆☆☆ |
| DETOX | ★★★★☆ |
| IMMUNITY | ★★★☆☆ |
| DIGESTION | ★★☆☆☆ |
| SKIN | ★★★☆☆ |

# 213 | salty sharp melon

3 sticks celery
½ melon
1 lime

Melon juice is so sweet and creamy – here the celery and lime lift it to a sharper plane.

**NUTRIENTS**

Beta-carotene, folic acid, vitamin C;
calcium, magnesium, manganese,
phosphorus, potassium, sodium,
sulphur

| | |
|---|---|
| ENERGY | ★★★☆☆ |
| DETOX | ★★★☆☆ |
| IMMUNITY | ★★★★☆ |
| DIGESTION | ☆☆☆☆☆ |
| SKIN | ★★★☆☆ |

# 214 | soft and sharp

3 sticks celery
2 pears
1 large bunch watercress

The sharp contrast between the pear and the watercress goes well with the fresh, salty celery in this pretty, green drink.

**NUTRIENTS**

Beta-carotene, folic acid, vitamin C,
vitamin E; calcium, iron, magnesium,
phosphorus, potassium, sodium,
sulphur

| | |
|---|---|
| ENERGY | ★★☆☆☆ |
| DETOX | ★★★★★ |
| IMMUNITY | ★★★★☆ |
| DIGESTION | ★★★☆☆ |
| SKIN | ★★★☆☆ |

# 215 | grape crunch

4 sticks celery
1 large bunch seedless grapes (about 50)

There's something about the sweetness of grapes that goes
fantastically well with celery. Use either green or red grapes,
although red are richer in antioxidants.

### NUTRIENTS

Folic acid, vitamin C, vitamin E;
calcium, manganese, phosphorus,
potassium, sodium, sulphur

| | |
|---|---|
| ENERGY | ★★★★☆ |
| DETOX | ★★★★☆ |
| IMMUNITY | ★★★☆☆ |
| DIGESTION | ★★☆☆☆ |
| SKIN | ★★★☆☆ |

# 216 | tricolore cruncher

3 sticks celery
3 tomatoes
1 small bunch parsley
1 handful watercress
$\frac{1}{2}$ lemon

Fresh and cleansing – with a kick from the watercress and lemon,
this is a delicious, salad-like combination.

### NUTRIENTS

Beta-carotene, biotin, folic acid,
vitamins B3, C and E; calcium, iron,
magnesium, manganese, phosphorus,
potassium, sodium, sulphur

| | |
|---|---|
| ENERGY | ★★☆☆☆ |
| DETOX | ★★★★☆ |
| IMMUNITY | ★★★☆☆ |
| DIGESTION | ☆☆☆☆☆ |
| SKIN | ★★★★★ |

## 217 | take heart

4 sticks celery
1 apple
1 handful blackcurrants
½ inch (1 cm) ginger root
1 tablespoon (15 ml) flaxseed (linseed) oil

Each of the ingredients in this bright
juice has properties that can help
support healthy blood pressure and
blood vessels – and it tastes great.

**NUTRIENTS**

Beta-carotene, biotin, folic acid,
vitamin C, vitamin E; calcium, magnesium,
manganese, phosphorus, potassium,
sodium, sulphur; essential fatty acids

| | |
|---|---|
| ENERGY | ★★★☆☆ |
| DETOX | ★★★★☆ |
| IMMUNITY | ★★★★☆ |
| DIGESTION | ★★☆☆☆ |
| SKIN | ★★★★☆ |

## 218 | chlorophyll crunch

3 sticks celery
3 carrots
1 bunch parsley

Creamy carrots, salty celery and perky parsley combine in this substantial
drink that is a good detoxifier and all-round immune-boosting tonic. You
really can taste the goodness.

**NUTRIENTS**

Beta-carotene, folic acid, vitamin B3,
vitamin C; calcium, iron, magnesium,
manganese, phosphorus, potassium,
sodium, sulphur

| | |
|---|---|
| ENERGY | ★★☆☆☆ |
| DETOX | ★★★★★ |
| IMMUNITY | ★★★★★ |
| DIGESTION | ★★★☆☆ |
| SKIN | ★★★★☆ |

## 219 | veggie cocktail

3 sticks celery
3 tomatoes
2 carrots
½ lemon

A sweet, pale orange vegetable juice – you could add
some parsley too if you want that green, cleansing taste.

**NUTRIENTS**
Beta-carotene, biotin, folic acid,
vitamin C; calcium, magnesium,
manganese, phosphorus, potassium,
sodium, sulphur

ENERGY ★★★★☆
DETOX ★★★☆☆
IMMUNITY ★★★★★
DIGESTION ★☆☆☆☆
SKIN ★★★★☆

## 220 | celery blood cleanser

3 sticks celery
1 apple
1 beet (beetroot)
1 teaspoon spirulina

You can hardly believe this is so good for you, it has such a fantastic
taste. Put in a little less beet if you're not a hardened fan. Shake the
spirulina with some of the juice in a jar before mixing in with the rest.

**NUTRIENTS**
Beta-carotene, folic acid, vitamins B1, B3,
B5, B6 and C; calcium, iron, magnesium,
manganese, phosphorus, potassium, sodium,
sulphur; protein, essential fatty acids

ENERGY ★★★☆☆
DETOX ★★★★★
IMMUNITY ★★★☆☆
DIGESTION ★★★★☆
SKIN ★★★★☆

# making
# smoothies
## chapter 3

Making a smoothie couldn't be easier – just prepare your ingredients (see pp.14–24), throw them into a blender and press "on".

In this chapter, fruity smoothies are thick drinks made from fresh fruits blended together with a little added fruit juice; and creamy smoothies are a richer, creamier drink because they contain yogurt. All of the creamy smoothie recipes list yogurt, but you can use milk or soy (soya) milk instead if you prefer a runnier drink. Either way, a creamy smoothie provides a rich source of protein.

Each recipe suggests which juice to add to help make your smoothie a drink, rather than a pudding, but feel free to experiment with different juices and different amounts according to your tastes and preferences. The recipes each make two generous portions, and provide a delicious, substantial drink, snack or even light meal for any time of the day.

# top tips

Below are a few reminders and helpful hints, tips and suggestions to enable you to get the most from your smoothie making.

1   Choose fruit for a smoothie at its peak of ripeness for the best taste and most goodness in a glass.

2   When adding juice to your smoothie, use fresh, home-made juice in preference to commercially produced juices (which often contain artificial sweeteners and other additives).

3   When adding juice to your smoothie, you don't have to stick rigidly to the one listed in the ingredients – try using whichever juice you have available rather than go without.

4   Add more or less juice to your smoothie, according to your own tastes and preferences to make a thicker or thinner drink.

5   For creamy smoothies, the recipes suggest using yogurt. For thinner, runnier drinks, use milk or a milk alternative made from soy (soya), rice or nuts.

6   Use soy (soya) yogurt or soy (soya) milk as a non-dairy alternative when making creamy smoothies.

7   For a more refreshing smoothie, blend a few crushed cubes of ice in with the other ingredients.

8   Any smoothie can be frozen to be eaten as a delicious popsicle (ice-lolly). Either use special popsicle moulds or ice cube trays.

9   Try adding some of the extra ingredients listed on pp.24–5 to give your smoothie an even greater healthy boost.

10  Even if you don't have all the fruits needed for a particular recipe, or the exact amounts, give it a try anyway and have some fun creating your own blends.

# 221 | pink banana

2 bananas
8 medium strawberries
10 tablespoons (150 ml) apple juice

This one is a summer favourite – best to use organic, fresh strawberries.

**NUTRIENTS**

Beta-carotene, biotin, folic acid,
vitamins B1, B3, B6 and C; calcium,
magnesium, phosphorus, potassium,
sulphur

| | |
|---|---|
| ENERGY | ★★★★★ |
| DETOX | ★☆☆☆☆ |
| IMMUNITY | ★★★☆☆ |
| DIGESTION | ★☆☆☆☆ |
| SKIN | ★★★☆☆ |

# 222 | green banana smoothie

1 banana
½ pineapple
8 tablespoons (120 ml) pineapple juice
2 tablespoons (30 ml) coconut milk
1 heaped teaspoon spirulina

The spirulina turns this delicious, pastel yellow drink into a green delight.

**NUTRIENTS**

Beta-carotene, folic acid, vitamins B1, B3, B6
and C; calcium, iron, magnesium, manganese,
phosphorus, potassium, sodium, sulphur;
protein, essential fatty acids

| | |
|---|---|
| ENERGY | ★★★★★ |
| DETOX | ★★★☆☆ |
| IMMUNITY | ★★★☆☆ |
| DIGESTION | ★★★★☆ |
| SKIN | ★★★☆☆ |

# 223 | green banana too

2 bananas
2 kiwi fruits
1 handful red seedless grapes
10 tablespoons (150 ml) apple juice

This one goes a pretty, green colour because of the delicious, tangy,
vitamin C-rich kiwi fruit.

**NUTRIENTS**

Beta-carotene, folic acid, vitamins B1, B3, B6,
C and E; calcium, magnesium, manganese,
phosphorus, potassium, sodium, sulphur

| | |
|---|---|
| ENERGY | ★★★★★ |
| DETOX | ★★★★☆ |
| IMMUNITY | ★★★★☆ |
| DIGESTION | ★★★☆☆ |
| SKIN | ★★★★☆ |

## 224 | banana sharp

2 bananas
1 pink grapefruit
8 tablespoons (120 ml) orange juice
juice of a lime

A great contrast between the tangy citrus and sweet banana.

### NUTRIENTS

Beta-carotene, folic acid, vitamins B1, B3,
B6 and C; calcium, magnesium, phosphorus,
potassium, sodium, sulphur

| | |
|---|---|
| ENERGY | ★★★★★ |
| DETOX | ★☆☆☆☆ |
| IMMUNITY | ★★★☆☆ |
| DIGESTION | ★☆☆☆☆ |
| SKIN | ★★★☆☆ |

## 225 | pink lady

2 bananas
2 handfuls raspberries
10 tablespoons (150 ml) cranberry juice

This one is certainly heaven-sent and gives a great energy boost too.

### NUTRIENTS

Beta-carotene, biotin, folic acid,
vitamins B1, B3, B6 and C; calcium, iron,
magnesium, manganese, phosphorus,
potassium, sodium, sulphur

| | |
|---|---|
| ENERGY | ★★★★★ |
| DETOX | ★☆☆☆☆ |
| IMMUNITY | ★★★☆☆ |
| DIGESTION | ★★☆☆☆ |
| SKIN | ★★★☆☆ |

## 226 | pure passion

3 bananas
4 passion fruits
10 tablespoons (150 ml) guava juice

Surely one of the most exquisite combinations of fruit ever.

### NUTRIENTS

Beta-carotene, folic acid, vitamins B1,
B3, B6 and C; calcium, iron, magnesium,
phosphorus, potassium, sodium, sulphur

| | |
|---|---|
| ENERGY | ★★★★★ |
| DETOX | ★☆☆☆☆ |
| IMMUNITY | ★★★☆☆ |
| DIGESTION | ★☆☆☆☆ |
| SKIN | ★★★☆☆ |

## 227 | black banana

2 bananas
2 heaped tablespoons blackcurrants
10 tablespoons (150 ml) apple juice (or the juice from
the blackcurrants, if they come from a can)

A wonderful contrast between the sweet banana and the
tangy blackcurrants. Use blackcurrants canned in natural
juice if you don't have fresh ones – a good standby to
keep in the cupboard in winter.

**NUTRIENTS**

Beta-carotene, biotin, vitamins B1,
B3, B6, C and E; calcium, iron,
magnesium, phosphorus,
potassium, sodium, sulphur

| | |
|---|---|
| ENERGY | ★★★★★ |
| DETOX | ★☆☆☆☆ |
| IMMUNITY | ★★★☆☆ |
| DIGESTION | ★☆☆☆☆ |
| SKIN | ★★★☆☆ |

## 228 | banana nectar

2 bananas
4 apricots
10 tablespoons (150 ml) apricot or apple juice

Nothing to do with nectarines – I always think the pulp or juice of apricots
conjures up the word nectar more than most fruits.

**NUTRIENTS**

Beta-carotene, folic acid, vitamins B1, B3, B6
and C; calcium, magnesium, phosphorus,
potassium, sulphur

| | |
|---|---|
| ENERGY | ★★★★★ |
| DETOX | ★☆☆☆☆ |
| IMMUNITY | ★★★☆☆ |
| DIGESTION | ★★☆☆☆ |
| SKIN | ★★★☆☆ |

## 229 | easy morning mash

2 bananas
1 pear
1 orange
8 tablespoons (120 ml) apple juice

Just reach into the fruit bowl and whiz it all up. Easy.

### NUTRIENTS

Beta-carotene, folic acid, vitamins B1,
B3, B6 and C; calcium, magnesium,
phosphorus, potassium, sulphur

| | |
|---|---|
| ENERGY | ★★★★★ |
| DETOX | ★☆☆☆☆ |
| IMMUNITY | ★★★☆☆ |
| DIGESTION | ★★☆☆☆ |
| SKIN | ★★☆☆☆ |

## 230 | banana pie

2 bananas
1 apple
1 handful blackberries (or blackcurrants)
10 tablespoons (150 ml) apple juice

Well, not literally, but I always think of the apple and blackberry
pie combination when the two are blended and they cut deliciously
through the dense flavour of the banana.

### NUTRIENTS

Beta-carotene, folic acid, vitamins B1,
B3, B5, B6, C and E; calcium, iron,
magnesium, phosphorus, potassium,
sodium, sulphur

| | |
|---|---|
| ENERGY | ★★★★★ |
| DETOX | ★☆☆☆☆ |
| IMMUNITY | ★★★☆☆ |
| DIGESTION | ★★☆☆☆ |
| SKIN | ★★☆☆☆ |

## 231 | tropical treat

1 banana
½ pineapple
½ papaya
8 tablespoons (120 ml) guava juice

Fancy being transported to a fresh fruit salad on a beach in Thailand?

**NUTRIENTS**

Beta-carotene, folic acid, vitamin B3, vitamin C; calcium, magnesium, manganese, phosphorus, potassium, sodium, sulphur

ENERGY ★★★★★
DETOX ★☆☆☆☆
IMMUNITY ★★★☆☆
DIGESTION ★★★★☆
SKIN ★★★☆☆

## 232 | peaches 'n' dream

2 bananas
2 peaches
2 tangerines
8 tablespoons (120 ml) orange juice

Juicy, ripe peaches (or nectarines) make this one a dream combination.

**NUTRIENTS**

Beta-carotene, folic acid, vitamins B1, B3, B6 and C; calcium, magnesium, phosphorus, potassium, sodium, sulphur

ENERGY ★★★★★
DETOX ★☆☆☆☆
IMMUNITY ★★★☆☆
DIGESTION ★★☆☆☆
SKIN ★★☆☆☆

## 233 | mellow bite

2 bananas
½ melon
8 tablespoons (120 ml) apple juice
juice of a lime

The contrasting mild melon and sharp lime make quite an impact on your tastebuds but are mellowed by the banana.

**NUTRIENTS**

Beta-carotene, folic acid, vitamins B1, B3, B6 and C; calcium, iron, magnesium, phosphorus, potassium, sodium, sulphur

ENERGY ★★★★★
DETOX ★☆☆☆☆
IMMUNITY ★★★☆☆
DIGESTION ★☆☆☆☆
SKIN ★★☆☆☆

## 234 | coconutty 'nana

2 bananas
$\frac{1}{2}$ pineapple
2 tablespoons (30 ml) coconut milk
8 tablespoons (120 ml) pineapple juice

If you're a fan of coconut, you'll love this one and the
way it transports you to a warm, palm-fringed beach.

**NUTRIENTS**

Beta-carotene, folic acid, vitamins B1,
B3, B6, C and E; calcium, magnesium,
manganese, phosphorus, potassium,
sodium, sulphur

| | |
|---|---|
| ENERGY | ★★★★★ |
| DETOX | ★☆☆☆☆ |
| IMMUNITY | ★★★☆☆ |
| DIGESTION | ★★★★☆ |
| SKIN | ★★☆☆☆ |

## 235 | regular banana

2 bananas
10 prunes (soaked and pitted)
$\frac{1}{2}$ teaspoon vanilla essence
10 tablespoons (150 ml) apple juice

You'd barely believe this was so good for keeping your guts
going, it tastes so delicious. Use particularly ripe bananas.

**NUTRIENTS**

Beta-carotene, folic acid, vitamins B1,
B3, B6 and C; calcium, magnesium,
phosphorus, potassium, sulphur

| | |
|---|---|
| ENERGY | ★★★★☆ |
| DETOX | ★☆☆☆☆ |
| IMMUNITY | ★★★☆☆ |
| DIGESTION | ★★★☆☆ |
| SKIN | ★★☆☆☆ |

## 236 | eve's delight

2 mangoes
2 apples
8 tablespoons (120 ml) apple juice

If she'd had anything to blend it with in Eden, surely it would have
been a juicy, ripe mango. This is one of my all-time favourite smoothies.

### NUTRIENTS

Beta-carotene, folic acid, vitamin C,
vitamin E; calcium, iron, magnesium,
phosphorus, potassium, sodium,
sulphur

| | |
|---|---|
| ENERGY | ★★★★★ |
| DETOX | ★☆☆☆☆ |
| IMMUNITY | ★★★★☆ |
| DIGESTION | ★★★★☆ |
| SKIN | ★★☆☆☆ |

## 237 | mango crush

2 mangoes
2 oranges
juice of a lime
8 tablespoons (120 ml) apple juice

One pure orange colour, two different tastes, one
result – a fabulous smoothie where the creamy, sweet
mango contrasts well with the tangy orange.

### NUTRIENTS

Beta-carotene, folic acid, vitamin C,
vitamin E; calcium, iron, magnesium,
phosphorus, potassium, sodium, sulphur

| | |
|---|---|
| ENERGY | ★★★★★ |
| DETOX | ★☆☆☆☆ |
| IMMUNITY | ★★★★★ |
| DIGESTION | ★☆☆☆☆ |
| SKIN | ★★★☆☆ |

## 238 | simple tropical

2 mangoes
1 banana
10 tablespoons (150 ml) orange juice

Dense and rich, this is a high energy blend. You can use pineapple juice as an alternative to the orange for an extra tropical touch.

**NUTRIENTS**

Beta-carotene, folic acid, vitamins B1, B3, B6, C and E; calcium, iron, magnesium, phosphorus, potassium, sodium, sulphur

| | |
|---|---|
| ENERGY | ★★★★★ |
| DETOX | ★☆☆☆☆ |
| IMMUNITY | ★★★☆☆ |
| DIGESTION | ★★☆☆☆ |
| SKIN | ★★★☆☆ |

## 239 | mango passion

2 mangoes
$\frac{1}{2}$ pineapple
2 passion fruits
8 tablespoons (120 ml) pineapple juice

I love any blend with passion fruit, but with pineapple and mango, mmm...

**NUTRIENTS**

Beta-carotene, folic acid, vitamins B3, C and E; calcium, iron, magnesium, manganese, phosphorus, potassium, sodium, sulphur

| | |
|---|---|
| ENERGY | ★★★★★ |
| DETOX | ★☆☆☆☆ |
| IMMUNITY | ★★★★☆ |
| DIGESTION | ★★★★☆ |
| SKIN | ★★★☆☆ |

## 240 | manilla

2 mangoes
4 tangerines
$\frac{1}{2}$ teaspoon vanilla essence
8 tablespoons (120 ml) orange juice

Somehow the vanilla makes this taste even sweeter.

**NUTRIENTS**

Beta-carotene, folic acid, vitamin C, vitamin E; calcium, iron, magnesium, phosphorus, potassium, sodium, sulphur

| | |
|---|---|
| ENERGY | ★★★★★ |
| DETOX | ★☆☆☆☆ |
| IMMUNITY | ★★★★★ |
| DIGESTION | ★☆☆☆☆ |
| SKIN | ★★★☆☆ |

## 241 | mango zingo

2 mangoes
1 grapefruit
$\frac{1}{4}$ inch (0.5 cm) grated ginger root
8 tablespoons (120 ml) apple juice

The slightly bitter grapefruit and spicy ginger blend beautifully with sweet, creamy mango to create this energy- and immunity-boosting drink.

**NUTRIENTS**

Beta-carotene, folic acid, vitamin C, vitamin E; calcium, iron, magnesium, phosphorus, potassium, sodium, sulphur

| | |
|---|---|
| ENERGY | ★★★★★ |
| DETOX | ★☆☆☆☆ |
| IMMUNITY | ★★★★★ |
| DIGESTION | ★★☆☆☆ |
| SKIN | ★★★☆☆ |

## 242 | summer mango special

2 mangoes
2 handfuls raspberries
juice of half a lemon
8 tablespoons (120 ml) apple juice

Just as those fantastic Indian mangoes are at the tail end of their season, the raspberries come in – catch this divine combination if you can, otherwise use any good mango.

**NUTRIENTS**

Beta-carotene, biotin, folic acid, vitamin C, vitamin E; calcium, iron, magnesium, manganese, phosphorus, potassium, sodium, sulphur

| | |
|---|---|
| ENERGY | ★★★★★ |
| DETOX | ★★☆☆☆ |
| IMMUNITY | ★★★☆☆ |
| DIGESTION | ★★☆☆☆ |
| SKIN | ★★☆☆☆ |

## 243 | tropical deluxe

2 mangoes
2 bananas
juice of a lime
8 tablespoons (120 ml) guava juice

There have to be very few, if any, smoothies that go down this well.

**NUTRIENTS**

Beta-carotene, folic acid, vitamins B1, B3, B6, C and E; calcium, iron, magnesium, phosphorus, potassium, sodium, sulphur

| | |
|---|---|
| ENERGY | ★★★★★ |
| DETOX | ★☆☆☆☆ |
| IMMUNITY | ★★★★☆ |
| DIGESTION | ★★☆☆☆ |
| SKIN | ★★★☆☆ |

## 244 | nectargo

2 mangoes
2 nectarines
1 orange
8 tablespoons (120 ml) orange juice

A triple-orange whammy with a taste to match. This is also an excellent booster blend for the body's defences.

### NUTRIENTS

Beta-carotene, folic acid, vitamin C, vitamin E; calcium, iron, magnesium, phosphorus, potassium, sodium, sulphur

| | |
|---|---|
| ENERGY | ★★★★★ |
| DETOX | ★☆☆☆☆ |
| IMMUNITY | ★★★★★ |
| DIGESTION | ★☆☆☆☆ |
| SKIN | ★★★★☆ |

## 245 | mango blues

2 mangoes
2 handfuls blueberries
juice of a lime
8 tablespoons (120 ml) apple juice

Tropic and temperate fruits kicking up a storm in frothy red.

### NUTRIENTS

Beta-carotene, biotin, folic acid, vitamins B1, B2, B6, C and E; calcium, chromium, iron, magnesium, phosphorus, potassium, sodium, sulphur

| | |
|---|---|
| ENERGY | ★★★★★ |
| DETOX | ★★☆☆☆ |
| IMMUNITY | ★★★★★ |
| DIGESTION | ★★☆☆☆ |
| SKIN | ★★★★☆ |

# 246 | pineapple classic

½ pineapple
2 bananas
2 passion fruits
8 tablespoons (120 ml) pineapple juice

An idyllic tropical combo.

**NUTRIENTS**

Beta-carotene, folic acid, vitamin B3,
vitamin C; calcium, iron, magnesium,
manganese, phosphorus, potassium,
sodium, sulphur

| ENERGY | ★★★★★ |
| DETOX | ★☆☆☆☆ |
| IMMUNITY | ★★★☆☆ |
| DIGESTION | ★★★☆☆ |
| SKIN | ★★★☆☆ |

# 247 | citrus pineapple

½ pineapple
2 oranges
juice of a lime
6 tablespoons (90 ml) orange juice

A blend of three tangy flavours to get your tastebuds singing.

**NUTRIENTS**

Beta-carotene, folic acid, vitamin C;
calcium, magnesium, manganese,
phosphorus, potassium, sodium

| ENERGY | ★★★★★ |
| DETOX | ★☆☆☆☆ |
| IMMUNITY | ★★★★☆ |
| DIGESTION | ★★☆☆☆ |
| SKIN | ★★☆☆☆ |

# 248 | pineapple zing

½ pineapple
1 grapefruit
¼ inch (0.5 cm) grated ginger root
8 tablespoons (120 ml) pineapple juice

If you don't use a sweet, pink grapefruit for this one, you'll be in
for a sharp surprise. You decide.

**NUTRIENTS**

Beta-carotene, folic acid, vitamin C;
calcium, magnesium, manganese,
phosphorus, potassium, sodium,
sulphur,

| ENERGY | ★★★★★ |
| DETOX | ★☆☆☆☆ |
| IMMUNITY | ★★★★☆ |
| DIGESTION | ★★★☆☆ |
| SKIN | ★★★☆☆ |

## 249 | summer refresher

$\frac{3}{4}$ pineapple
1 handful raspberries
5–6 fresh mint leaves
8 tablespoons (120 ml) pineapple juice

A tropic-temperate blend of fruits lifted even higher with the refreshing mint.

**NUTRIENTS**

Beta-carotene, biotin, folic acid,
vitamin C; calcium, magnesium,
manganese, phosphorus, potassium,
sodium, sulphur

| | |
|---|---|
| ENERGY | ★★★★★ |
| DETOX | ★☆☆☆☆ |
| IMMUNITY | ★★★☆☆ |
| DIGESTION | ★★★☆☆ |
| SKIN | ★★★☆☆ |

## 250 | pastel perfect

$\frac{1}{2}$ pineapple
3 kiwi fruits
8 tablespoons (120 ml) pineapple juice

A delicious mix that can be sharp on the tongue if the fruits aren't nice and ripe, so pick your moment well.

**NUTRIENTS**

Beta-carotene, folic acid, vitamin C;
calcium, magnesium, manganese,
phosphorus, potassium, sodium

| | |
|---|---|
| ENERGY | ★★★★★ |
| DETOX | ★★☆☆☆ |
| IMMUNITY | ★★★★☆ |
| DIGESTION | ★★★☆☆ |
| SKIN | ★★★☆☆ |

## 251 | malibu mix

1 pineapple
2 tablespoons (30 ml) coconut milk
$\frac{1}{2}$ teaspoon vanilla essence
juice of $\frac{1}{2}$ lemon
5 tablespoons (75 ml) pineapple juice

Sit back and enjoy the sunshine. Well, perhaps the central heating ... . Either way, it's very good and will transport you to tropical climes.

**NUTRIENTS**

Beta-carotene, folic acid, vitamin C,
vitamin E; calcium, magnesium,
manganese, phosphorus, potassium,
sodium, sulphur

| | |
|---|---|
| ENERGY | ★★★★★ |
| DETOX | ★★☆☆☆ |
| IMMUNITY | ★★☆☆☆ |
| DIGESTION | ★★★☆☆ |
| SKIN | ★★☆☆☆ |

# 252 | pineberry

$\frac{1}{2}$ pineapple
1 handful cranberries
1 handful strawberries
8 tablespoons (120 ml) pineapple juice

The sharp taste of the cranberries is well balanced
by the sweetness of all the other ingredients.

**NUTRIENTS**

Beta-carotene, biotin, folic acid,
vitamin C; calcium, iron, magnesium,
manganese, phosphorus, potassium,
sodium, sulphur

| | |
|---|---|
| ENERGY | ★★★★★ |
| DETOX | ★★☆☆☆ |
| IMMUNITY | ★★★★☆ |
| DIGESTION | ★★☆☆☆ |
| SKIN | ★★★☆☆ |

# 253 | apple squared

$\frac{1}{2}$ pineapple
2 apples
8 tablespoons (120 ml) apple juice

I was surprised at how well this combination worked out! Use a
relatively sweet apple variety, such as Pink Lady or Empire, for
the perfect contrast.

**NUTRIENTS**

Beta-carotene, folic acid, vitamin C;
calcium, magnesium, manganese,
phosphorus, potassium, sodium,
sulphur

| | |
|---|---|
| ENERGY | ★★★★★ |
| DETOX | ★☆☆☆☆ |
| IMMUNITY | ★★★☆☆ |
| DIGESTION | ★★★★☆ |
| SKIN | ★★★☆☆ |

## 254 | papaya pure

2 papayas
juice of a lime
8 tablespoons (120 ml) apple juice

This, the first of three Thai-inspired recipes, is pure Thailand in a glass –
whenever you buy a slice of fresh papaya from a street stall in this tropical
country, it is always served with a wedge of lime.

### NUTRIENTS

Beta-carotene, folic acid, vitamin C;
calcium, magnesium, phosphorus,
potassium, sodium, sulphur

| | |
|---|---|
| ENERGY | ★★★★★ |
| DETOX | ★★★★☆ |
| IMMUNITY | ★★★★☆ |
| DIGESTION | ★★★★☆ |
| SKIN | ★★★★☆ |

## 255 | papaya salad

1 papaya
$\frac{1}{4}$ pineapple
1 slice watermelon
1 banana
8 tablespoons (120 ml) pineapple juice

This classic combo served to tropical-fruit-hungry foreigners for breakfast
in Thailand is a delicious smoothie in any corner of the globe.

### NUTRIENTS

Beta-carotene, folic acid, vitamins B1,
B3, B5, B6 and C; calcium, magnesium,
manganese, phosphorus, potassium,
sodium, sulphur

| | |
|---|---|
| ENERGY | ★★★★★ |
| DETOX | ★★★☆☆ |
| IMMUNITY | ★★★★☆ |
| DIGESTION | ★★★★☆ |
| SKIN | ★★★★☆ |

## 256 | identity crisis

1 papaya
3 tangerines
8 tablespoons (120 ml) orange juice

In Thailand, "oranges" are usually green and taste like tangerines.
Whatever … this is a wonderfully refreshing blend.

### NUTRIENTS

Beta-carotene, folic acid, vitamin C;
calcium, magnesium, phosphorus,
potassium, sodium

| | |
|---|---|
| ENERGY | ★★★★★ |
| DETOX | ★☆☆☆☆ |
| IMMUNITY | ★★★★★ |
| DIGESTION | ★★☆☆☆ |
| SKIN | ★★★☆☆ |

# 257 | heaven scent

1 papaya
1 grapefruit
1 handful raspberries
juice of a lime
8 tablespoons (120 ml) grapefruit juice

Quite a magnificent combination of tastes.

**NUTRIENTS**

Beta-carotene, biotin, folic acid,
vitamin C; calcium, magnesium,
manganese, phosphorus, potassium,
sodium, sulphur

| | |
|---|---|
| ENERGY | ★★★★★ |
| DETOX | ★☆☆☆☆ |
| IMMUNITY | ★★★★★ |
| DIGESTION | ★☆☆☆☆ |
| SKIN | ★★★★☆ |

# 258 | globe trotter

1 papaya
2 kiwi fruits
1 pear
8 tablespoons (120 ml) apple juice

This one is certainly a sign of the times — fruit from around the world
in one big taste.

**NUTRIENTS**

Beta-carotene, folic acid, vitamin C;
calcium, magnesium, phosphorus,
potassium, sodium, sulphur

| | |
|---|---|
| ENERGY | ★★★★★ |
| DETOX | ★☆☆☆☆ |
| IMMUNITY | ★★★★☆ |
| DIGESTION | ★★★☆☆ |
| SKIN | ★★★★☆ |

## 259 | supreme strawberry

2 handfuls strawberries
2 oranges
8 tablespoons (120 ml) guava juice

The most popular berry just got even better.

### NUTRIENTS

Beta-carotene, folic acid, biotin,
vitamin B3, vitamin C; calcium,
magnesium, phosphorus, potassium,
sodium, sulphur

| | |
|---|---|
| ENERGY | ★★★★★ |
| DETOX | ★☆☆☆☆ |
| IMMUNITY | ★★★★★ |
| DIGESTION | ☆☆☆☆☆ |
| SKIN | ★★★★☆ |

## 260 | strawblend classic

2 handfuls strawberries
1 banana
$\frac{1}{4}$ pineapple
8 tablespoons (120 ml) pineapple juice

Classic favourites, strawberries and banana, with a touch
of tang from the tropics create this fabulous staple blend.

### NUTRIENTS

Beta-carotene, biotin, folic acid,
vitamins B1, B3, B6 and C; calcium,
magnesium, manganese, phosphorus,
potassium, sodium, sulphur

| | |
|---|---|
| ENERGY | ★★★★★ |
| DETOX | ★☆☆☆☆ |
| IMMUNITY | ★★★★☆ |
| DIGESTION | ★★☆☆☆ |
| SKIN | ★★★★☆ |

## 261 | peachy strawbs

2 handfuls strawberries
3 peaches (or nectarines)
juice of one lime
8 tablespoons (120 ml) orange juice

Summer delight in a glass, and laden with antioxidants for better
immunity and healthy skin.

### NUTRIENTS

Beta-carotene, biotin, folic acid,
vitamin B3, vitamin C; calcium,
magnesium, phosphorus, potassium,
sodium, sulphur

| | |
|---|---|
| ENERGY | ★★★★★ |
| DETOX | ★★☆☆☆ |
| IMMUNITY | ★★★★★ |
| DIGESTION | ☆☆☆☆☆ |
| SKIN | ★★★★★ |

## 262 | pink berry crush

2 handfuls raspberries
2 handfuls strawberries
1 orange
3 or 4 fresh mint leaves
8 tablespoons (120 ml) orange juice

An easy summer favourite with a hint of mint.

**NUTRIENTS**

Beta-carotene, biotin, folic acid,
vitamin C; calcium, magnesium,
manganese, phosphorus, potassium,
sodium, sulphur

| | |
|---|---|
| ENERGY | ★★★★★ |
| DETOX | ★★☆☆☆ |
| IMMUNITY | ★★★★★ |
| DIGESTION | ★☆☆☆☆ |
| SKIN | ★★★★★ |

## 263 | citrus strawbs

2 handfuls strawberries
1 pink grapefruit
2 oranges
6 tablespoons (90 ml) orange juice

Another strawberry blend that'll have you coming back for more and more.

**NUTRIENTS**

Beta-carotene, biotin, folic acid,
vitamin C; calcium, magnesium,
phosphorus, potassium, sulphur

| | |
|---|---|
| ENERGY | ★★★★★ |
| DETOX | ★★☆☆☆ |
| IMMUNITY | ★★★★☆ |
| DIGESTION | ☆☆☆☆☆ |
| SKIN | ★★★☆☆ |

## 264 | berry bonanza II

1 handful raspberries
1 handful strawberries
1 handful blueberries
1 handful blackberries
8 tablespoons (120 ml) apple juice

Just use every type of berry they've got at the shop to create this high-energy, immunity-boosting combo.

**NUTRIENTS**

Beta-carotene, biotin, folic acid,
vitamins B1, B2, B6, C and E; calcium,
chromium, iron, magnesium, manganese,
phosphorus, potassium, sodium, sulphur

| | |
|---|---|
| ENERGY | ★★★★★ |
| DETOX | ★★☆☆☆ |
| IMMUNITY | ★★★★★ |
| DIGESTION | ★☆☆☆☆ |
| SKIN | ★★★★☆ |

## 265 | blue healer

1 handful blueberries
1 handful blackberries
1 handful blackcurrants
1 banana
10 tablespoons (150 ml) apple juice

Named after a boisterous breed of dog in Australia, this is a rich mix.

**NUTRIENTS**

Beta-carotene, biotin, folic acid,
vitamins B1, B2, B3, B5, B6, C and E;
calcium, chromium, iron, magnesium,
manganese, phosphorus, potassium,
sodium, sulphur

| | |
|---|---|
| ENERGY | ★★★★★ |
| DETOX | ★☆☆☆☆ |
| IMMUNITY | ★★★★★ |
| DIGESTION | ★★☆☆☆ |
| SKIN | ★★★★☆ |

## 266 | apple and black

2 handfuls blackberries
1 handful blackcurrants
2 apples
10 tablespoons (150 ml) apple juice

It's that favourite pie or crumble combination again, without the topping.

**NUTRIENTS**

Beta-carotene, biotin, folic acid,
vitamins B5, C and E; calcium, iron,
magnesium, phosphorus, potassium,
sodium, sulphur

| | |
|---|---|
| ENERGY | ★★★★★ |
| DETOX | ★☆☆☆☆ |
| IMMUNITY | ★★★★☆ |
| DIGESTION | ★★☆☆☆ |
| SKIN | ★★★★★ |

## 267 | cranapple crush

2 handfuls raspberries
1 handful cranberries
2 apples
10 tablespoons (150 ml) apple juice

Contrasting berries and sweet apples make a delicious drink.

**NUTRIENTS**

Beta-carotene, biotin, folic acid, vitamin C;
calcium, iron, magnesium, manganese,
phosphorus, potassium, sodium, sulphur

| | |
|---|---|
| ENERGY | ★★★★★ |
| DETOX | ★★☆☆☆ |
| IMMUNITY | ★★★★★ |
| DIGESTION | ☆☆☆☆☆ |
| SKIN | ★★★☆☆ |

# 268 | panana

3 peaches (or nectarines)
2 bananas
10 tablespoons (150 ml) apple juice

Creamy and sweet – a complete treat.

## NUTRIENTS

Beta-carotene, folic acid, vitamins B1, B3,
B6 and C; calcium, magnesium, phosphorus,
potassium, sodium, sulphur

| | |
|---|---|
| ENERGY | ★★★★★ |
| DETOX | ★☆☆☆☆ |
| IMMUNITY | ★★★★☆ |
| DIGESTION | ★★★☆☆ |
| SKIN | ★★★★☆ |

# 269 | peach melba

3 peaches (or nectarines)
1 banana
1 handful raspberries
10 tablespoons (150 ml) apple juice

An exquisite combination bursting with energy and taste.

## NUTRIENTS

Beta-carotene, biotin, folic acid,
vitamins B1, B3, B6 and C; calcium,
magnesium, manganese, phosphorus,
potassium, sodium, sulphur

| | |
|---|---|
| ENERGY | ★★★★★ |
| DETOX | ★☆☆☆☆ |
| IMMUNITY | ★★★★☆ |
| DIGESTION | ★★☆☆☆ |
| SKIN | ★★★☆☆ |

# 270 | summer sunset

3 peaches (or nectarines)
2 handfuls strawberries
10 tablespoons (150 ml) guava juice

You won't be able to stop drinking this one – heaven on a summer's day.

## NUTRIENTS

Beta-carotene, biotin, folic acid,
vitamin B3, vitamin C; calcium,
magnesium, phosphorus, potassium,
sodium, sulphur

| | |
|---|---|
| ENERGY | ★★★★★ |
| DETOX | ★☆☆☆☆ |
| IMMUNITY | ★★★★★ |
| DIGESTION | ☆☆☆☆☆ |
| SKIN | ★★★★★ |

## 271 | creamy orange dream

3 peaches (or nectarines)
1 mango
1 orange
8 tablespoons (120 ml) orange juice

Three different orange-coloured fruit, with wonderfully
contrasting tastes and textures.

**NUTRIENTS**
Beta-carotene, folic acid, vitamin B3,
vitamin C; calcium, iron, magnesium,
phosphorus, potassium, sodium, sulphur

ENERGY      ★★★★★
DETOX       ★☆☆☆☆
IMMUNITY    ★★★★★
DIGESTION   ★☆☆☆☆
SKIN        ★★★★★

## 272 | orangicot

5 apricots
2 oranges
8 tablespoons (120 ml) orange juice

Tangy and refreshing, with creamy apricots to take the edge
off the sharper oranges. Brimming with antioxidants.

**NUTRIENTS**
Beta-carotene, folic acid,
vitamins B1, B3, B5 and C; calcium,
magnesium, phosphorus, potassium,
sulphur

ENERGY      ★★★★★
DETOX       ★☆☆☆☆
IMMUNITY    ★★★★★
DIGESTION   ★☆☆☆☆
SKIN        ★★★★★

## 273 | apricot zinger

5 apricots
2 pears
$\frac{1}{4}$ inch (0.5 cm) grated ginger root
10 tablespoons (150 ml) apple juice

A surprising combination which blends beautifully thanks to the hot ginger contrasting with the rich, sweeter apricots.

**NUTRIENTS**

Beta-carotene, folic acid, vitamins B3, B5 and C; calcium, magnesium, phosphorus, potassium, sulphur

| | |
|---|---|
| ENERGY | ★★★★★ |
| DETOX | ★☆☆☆☆ |
| IMMUNITY | ★★★★★ |
| DIGESTION | ★★★☆☆ |
| SKIN | ★★★★★ |

## 274 | sweet 'n' smooth

10 apricots
juice of half a lime
10 tablespoons (150 ml) prune juice

The sweetness of these two combined is fantastic, not to mention good for keeping your guts going.

**NUTRIENTS**

Beta-carotene, folic acid, vitamins B3, B5 and C; calcium, magnesium, phosphorus, potassium, sulphur

| | |
|---|---|
| ENERGY | ★★★★★ |
| DETOX | ★☆☆☆☆ |
| IMMUNITY | ★★★★★ |
| DIGESTION | ★★★★★ |
| SKIN | ★★★★★ |

## 275 | pure watermelon

1 small watermelon (or 4 thick slices)

The fruit, the whole fruit and nothing but the fruit. The ground-up seeds add a nutty, not to mention nutritious, touch.

**NUTRIENTS**

Beta-carotene, folic acid, vitamin B5, vitamin C; calcium, magnesium, phosphorus, potassium, sodium

| | |
|---|---|
| ENERGY | ★★★★★ |
| DETOX | ★★★★☆ |
| IMMUNITY | ★★★★★ |
| DIGESTION | ★★☆☆☆ |
| SKIN | ★★★★★ |

## 276 | watermelon crush

$\frac{1}{2}$ small watermelon (or 2 thick slices)
2 handfuls raspberries

A tastebud sensation, and as for the colour…

**NUTRIENTS**

Beta-carotene, biotin, folic acid, vitamin B5, vitamin C; calcium, magnesium, manganese, phosphorus, potassium, sodium, sulphur

| | |
|---|---|
| ENERGY | ★★★★★ |
| DETOX | ★★☆☆☆ |
| IMMUNITY | ★★★★★ |
| DIGESTION | ★☆☆☆☆ |
| SKIN | ★★★★★ |

## 277 | creamy cooler

$\frac{1}{2}$ small watermelon (or 2 thick slices)
1 mango

Bubbling, refreshing and sweet – you can only swallow this down in huge, noisy, full-of-goodness gulps.

**NUTRIENTS**

Beta-carotene, folic acid, vitamins B5, C and E; calcium, iron, magnesium, phosphorus, potassium, sodium, sulphur

| | |
|---|---|
| ENERGY | ★★★★★ |
| DETOX | ★☆☆☆☆ |
| IMMUNITY | ★★★★☆ |
| DIGESTION | ★★☆☆☆ |
| SKIN | ★★★★☆ |

# 278 | melon zinger

$\frac{1}{2}$ melon
$\frac{1}{2}$ pineapple
$\frac{1}{4}$ inch (0.5 cm) grated ginger root

There's something about this blend that makes the result infinitely greater than the sum of its already fantastic parts.

### NUTRIENTS

| | | |
|---|---|---|
| Beta-carotene, folic acid, vitamin C; | ENERGY | ★★★★★ |
| calcium, magnesium, manganese, | DETOX | ★★☆☆☆ |
| phosphorus, potassium, sodium, | IMMUNITY | ★★★★☆ |
| sulphur | DIGESTION | ★★★★☆ |
| | SKIN | ★★★★☆ |

# 279 | green sensation

$\frac{1}{2}$ melon
2 kiwi fruits
1 pear
juice of half a lime
4 tablespoons (60 ml) apple juice

Three refreshing fruits blended with juice to make a kicking smoothie.

### NUTRIENTS

| | | |
|---|---|---|
| Beta-carotene, folic acid, vitamin C; | ENERGY | ★★★★★ |
| calcium, magnesium, phosphorus, | DETOX | ★★★☆☆ |
| potassium, sodium, sulphur | IMMUNITY | ★★★★☆ |
| | DIGESTION | ★★☆☆☆ |
| | SKIN | ★★★★☆ |

# 280 | melon sour

1 melon
juice of 2 limes
1 stick celery (with string well removed)
5–6 fresh mint leaves
4 tablespoons (60 ml) apple juice

A great, refreshing cocktail to awaken those sour tastebuds.

### NUTRIENTS

| | | |
|---|---|---|
| Beta-carotene, folic acid, vitamin C; | ENERGY | ★★★★★ |
| calcium, magnesium, phosphorus, | DETOX | ★★☆☆☆ |
| potassium, sodium, sulphur | IMMUNITY | ★★★★☆ |
| | DIGESTION | ☆☆☆☆☆ |
| | SKIN | ★★★☆☆ |

## 281 | creamy pure banana

2 bananas
5 tablespoons (75 ml) natural yogurt
10 tablespoons (150 ml) pineapple juice

Probably the original smoothie – bananas just ask to be made up into
a thick, creamy blend like this.

### NUTRIENTS

Beta-carotene, folic acid, vitamins B1,
B3, B6 and C; calcium, magnesium,
manganese, phosphorus, potassium,
sulphur, zinc; protein

| | |
|---|---|
| ENERGY | ★★★★☆ |
| DETOX | ☆☆☆☆☆ |
| IMMUNITY | ★★☆☆☆ |
| DIGESTION | ★★★★☆ |
| SKIN | ★★★☆☆ |

## 282 | creamy bananacot

2 bananas
4 apricots
5 tablespoons (75 ml) natural yogurt
10 tablespoons (150 ml) apricot or apple juice

When an apricot is ripe, it is food from the heavens.
You can make this in winter with apricots canned in juice.

### NUTRIENTS

Beta-carotene, folic acid, vitamins B1,
B3, B5, B6 and C; calcium, magnesium,
phosphorus, potassium, sulphur,
zinc; protein

| | |
|---|---|
| ENERGY | ★★★★☆ |
| DETOX | ☆☆☆☆☆ |
| IMMUNITY | ★★★☆☆ |
| DIGESTION | ★★★★☆ |
| SKIN | ★★★☆☆ |

# 283 | creamy black banana

1 banana
2 heaped tablespoons blackcurrants
5 tablespoons (75 ml) natural yogurt
10 tablespoons (150 ml) apple juice (or the juice from the
blackcurrants, if they come from a can)

This is my all-time favourite combination – the rich banana and tangy blackcurrants.
You can even make it throughout the winter using blackcurrants canned in natural
juice. Try crunching on the blackcurrant seeds as they are full of healthy oils.

**NUTRIENTS**

Beta-carotene, biotin, vitamins B1, B3, B5,
B6, C and E; calcium, magnesium, phosphorus,
potassium, sodium, sulphur, zinc; protein

| | |
|---|---|
| ENERGY | ★★★★☆ |
| DETOX | ☆☆☆☆☆ |
| IMMUNITY | ★★★★☆ |
| DIGESTION | ★★★☆☆ |
| SKIN | ★★★★☆ |

# 284 | creamy pink banana

1 banana
2 handfuls strawberries
5 tablespoons (75 ml) natural yogurt
8 tablespoons (120 ml) apple juice

Another favourite combination of mine – best in the summer with juicy, fresh,
flavoursome, organic strawberries.

**NUTRIENTS**

Beta-carotene, biotin, folic acid,
vitamins B1, B3, B6 and C; calcium,
magnesium, phosphorus, potassium,
sulphur, zinc; protein

| | |
|---|---|
| ENERGY | ★★★★☆ |
| DETOX | ☆☆☆☆☆ |
| IMMUNITY | ★★★★☆ |
| DIGESTION | ★★★☆☆ |
| SKIN | ★★★★☆ |

# 285 | creamy green banana

1 banana
$\frac{1}{4}$ pineapple
1 heaped teaspoon spirulina
5 tablespoons (75 ml) natural yogurt
6 tablespoons (90 ml) pineapple juice

This isn't to say you should use green bananas, but you turn a pale yellow
smoothie into a pastel green by adding the spirulina.

**NUTRIENTS**

Beta-carotene, folic acid, vitamins B1,
B3, B5, B6 and C; calcium, iron, magnesium,
manganese, phosphorus, potassium, sodium,
sulphur, zinc; protein, essential fatty acids

| | |
|---|---|
| ENERGY | ★★★★☆ |
| DETOX | ★★★☆☆ |
| IMMUNITY | ★★★☆☆ |
| DIGESTION | ★★★★☆ |
| SKIN | ★★☆☆☆ |

## 286 | tropical tang

1 banana
½ mango
½ pineapple
4 tablespoons (50 ml) pineapple juice
5 tablespoons (75 ml) natural yogurt

This one reminds me of my first backpacking trip to an idyllic beach in Thailand when smoothies were only on the menu for a couple of hours a day – when the generator was turned on and the blender could be powered up.

**NUTRIENTS**

Beta-carotene, folic acid, vitamins B1, B3, B6, C and E; calcium, iron, magnesium, manganese, phosphorus, potassium, sodium, sulphur, zinc; protein

| | |
|---|---|
| ENERGY | ★★★★☆ |
| DETOX | ★☆☆☆☆ |
| IMMUNITY | ★★★★☆ |
| DIGESTION | ★★★★☆ |
| SKIN | ★★★☆☆ |

## 287 | vanilla banana

2 bananas
8 rehydrated prunes
3 drops vanilla essence
5 tablespoons (75 ml) natural yogurt
6 tablespoons (90 ml) pineapple juice

This turns out a tasty, very sweet smoothie. If you don't have any prunes to hand or don't like them, use dried apricots instead. Both are best left to soak overnight first.

**NUTRIENTS**

Beta-carotene, folic acid, vitamins B1, B3, B6 and C; calcium, magnesium, manganese, phosphorus, potassium, sodium, sulphur, zinc; protein

| | |
|---|---|
| ENERGY | ★★★★★ |
| DETOX | ★☆☆☆☆ |
| IMMUNITY | ★★★★☆ |
| DIGESTION | ★★★★☆ |
| SKIN | ★★★☆☆ |

## 288 | creamy passion

2 bananas
4 passion fruits
5 tablespoons (75 ml) natural yogurt
10 tablespoons (150 ml) guava juice

Surely one of the most exquisite combinations of fruit ever, bound up with creamy yogurt into a thick meal in itself.

**NUTRIENTS**

Beta-carotene, folic acid, vitamin B1, B3, B6 and C; calcium, iron, magnesium, phosphorus, potassium, sodium, sulphur; protein

| | |
|---|---|
| ENERGY | ★★★★☆ |
| DETOX | ☆☆☆☆☆ |
| IMMUNITY | ★★★☆☆ |
| DIGESTION | ★★★☆☆ |
| SKIN | ★★☆☆☆ |

# 289 | banana heaven

2 bananas
4 dates (pitted)
1 teaspoon cocoa powder
$\frac{1}{2}$ teaspoon vanilla essence
1 teaspoon honey
1 teaspoon tahini
5 tablespoons (75 ml) natural yogurt
10 tablespoons (150 ml) pineapple juice

Unbelievably good, you'll wonder whether you're actually drinking a wickedly rich ice cream, laden with fat and calories.

## NUTRIENTS

Beta-carotene, folic acid, vitamins B1, B3, B6 and C; calcium, magnesium, phosphorus, potassium, sulphur, zinc; protein, essential fatty acids

ENERGY    ★★★★★
DETOX     ☆☆☆☆☆
IMMUNITY  ★★★☆☆
DIGESTION ★★★☆☆
SKIN      ★★★★☆

# 290 | peachy banana dream

2 bananas
2 peaches
2 tangerines
5 tablespoons (75 ml) natural yogurt
8 tablespoons (120 ml) orange juice

Juicy, ripe peaches (or nectarines) make this one a dream combination, full of energy, with the creaminess offset by the citrus.

## NUTRIENTS

Beta-carotene, folic acid, vitamins B1, B3, B6 and C; calcium, magnesium, phosphorus, potassium, sodium, sulphur; zinc, protein

ENERGY    ★★★★☆
DETOX     ★☆☆☆☆
IMMUNITY  ★★★★☆
DIGESTION ★★★☆☆
SKIN      ★★★☆☆

## 291 | creamy pure mango

2 mangoes
$\frac{1}{4}$ teaspoon ground cardamom
5 tablespoons (75 ml) natural yogurt
6 tablespoons (90 ml) pineapple juice

Dense and rich, this is a high energy blend, with a hint of my favourite spice. Just leave it out if you don't like cardamom.

### NUTRIENTS

Beta-carotene, folic acid, vitamin C, vitamin E; calcium, iron, magnesium, manganese, phosphorus, potassium, sodium, sulphur, zinc; protein

| | |
|---|---|
| ENERGY | ★★★★☆ |
| DETOX | ★★☆☆☆ |
| IMMUNITY | ★★★★☆ |
| DIGESTION | ★★★☆☆ |
| SKIN | ★★★☆☆ |

## 292 | magical mango

1 mango
1 banana
5 tablespoons (75 ml) natural yogurt
10 tablespoons (150 ml) orange juice

Creamy and sweet – free transport to the tropics included.

### NUTRIENTS

Beta-carotene, folic acid, vitamins B1, B3, B6, C and E; calcium, iron, magnesium, phosphorus, potassium, sodium, sulphur, zinc; protein

| | |
|---|---|
| ENERGY | ★★★★☆ |
| DETOX | ☆☆☆☆☆ |
| IMMUNITY | ★★★☆☆ |
| DIGESTION | ★★★☆☆ |
| SKIN | ★★★☆☆ |

## 293 | mango mango

2 mangoes
5 tablespoons (75 ml) natural yogurt
6 tablespoons (90 ml) pineapple juice

One of the fruits that was just made to be blended with yogurt.

### NUTRIENTS

Beta carotene, folic acid, vitamin C, vitamin E; calcium, iron, magnesium, manganese, phosphorus, potassium, sodium, sulphur, zinc; protein

| | |
|---|---|
| ENERGY | ★★★★☆ |
| DETOXING | ★☆☆☆☆ |
| IMMUNITY | ★★★★☆ |
| DIGESTION | ★★★★☆ |
| SKIN | ★★★☆☆ |

## 294 | pango mango

2 mangoes
2 peaches
½ teaspoon vanilla essence
5 tablespoons (75 ml) natural yogurt
8 tablespoons (120 ml) orange juice

Two fantastically fruity orange fruits taken to another realm with the hint of vanilla, which seems to make it even sweeter.

**NUTRIENTS**

Beta-carotene, folic acid, vitamins B3, C and E; calcium, iron, magnesium, phosphorus, potassium, sodium, sulphur, zinc; protein

| | |
|---|---|
| ENERGY | ★★★★☆ |
| DETOX | ★☆☆☆☆ |
| IMMUNITY | ★★★★☆ |
| DIGESTION | ★★★☆☆ |
| SKIN | ★★★★☆ |

## 295 | pinky mango

2 mangoes
2 handfuls raspberries
juice of half a lemon
5 tablespoons (75 ml) natural yogurt
8 tablespoons (120 ml) apple juice

Who said East is East and West is West – the twain meet superbly here.

**NUTRIENTS**

Beta-carotene, biotin, folic acid, vitamin C, vitmain E; calcium, iron, magnesium, manganese, phosphorus, potassium, sodium, sulphur, zinc; protein

| | |
|---|---|
| ENERGY | ★★★★☆ |
| DETOX | ★☆☆☆☆ |
| IMMUNITY | ★★★★☆ |
| DIGESTION | ★★★☆☆ |
| SKIN | ★★★☆☆ |

## 296 | tropical mango medley

1 mango
½ pineapple
1 banana
1 passion fruit
5 tablespoons (75 ml) natural yogurt
6 tablespoons (90 ml) pineapple juice

A delicious, creamy drink redolent of breakfast on a palm-fringed beach.

**NUTRIENTS**

Beta carotene, folic acid, vitamins B1, B3, B6, C and E; calcium, iron, magnesium, manganese, phosphorus, potassium, sodium, sulphur, zinc; protein

| | |
|---|---|
| ENERGY | ★★★★☆ |
| DETOX | ★☆☆☆☆ |
| IMMUNITY | ★★★★☆ |
| DIGESTION | ★★★★☆ |
| SKIN | ★★★☆☆ |

## 297 | cocogo

2 mangoes
1 tablespoon (15 ml) coconut milk
½ teaspoon vanilla essence
5 tablespoons (75 ml) natural yogurt
6 tablespoons (90 ml) pineapple juice

A sweet, creamy drink with the tropical taste of coconut. Another one to transport you to sunny climes.

### NUTRIENTS

Beta-carotene, folic acid, vitamin C, vitamin E; calcium, iron, magnesium, phosphorus, potassium, sodium, sulphur, zinc; protein,

| | |
|---|---|
| ENERGY | ★★★★☆ |
| DETOX | ★☆☆☆☆ |
| IMMUNITY | ★★★★☆ |
| DIGESTION | ★★★☆☆ |
| SKIN | ★★★☆☆ |

## 298 | berry mango

1 mango
1 handful strawberries
¼ pineapple
5 tablespoons (75 ml) natural yogurt
6 tablespoons (90 ml) pineapple juice

The tangy pineapple contrasts deliciously with the creamy mango and sweet strawberries.

### NUTRIENTS

Beta-carotene, folic acid, vitamin C, vitamin E; calcium, iron, magnesium, manganese, phosphorus, potassium, sodium, sulphur, zinc; protein

| | |
|---|---|
| ENERGY | ★★★★☆ |
| DETOX | ★☆☆☆☆ |
| IMMUNITY | ★★★★☆ |
| DIGESTION | ★★★★☆ |
| SKIN | ★★★★☆ |

# 299 | flecked mango

2 mangoes
2 handfuls blueberries
5 tablespoons (75 ml) natural yogurt
8 tablespoons (120 ml) apple juice

I love the flecks of blue that the skins of the berries dot throughout
this drink, let alone the sublime taste they produce.

**NUTRIENTS**

Beta-carotene, biotin, folic acid,
vitamins B1, B2, B6, C and E;
calcium, chromium, iron, magnesium,
phosphorus, potassium, sodium,
sulphur, zinc; protein

| | |
|---|---|
| ENERGY | ★★★★☆ |
| DETOX | ★☆☆☆☆ |
| IMMUNITY | ★★★★☆ |
| DIGESTION | ★★★☆☆ |
| SKIN | ★★★☆☆ |

# 300 | passionate about mangoes

2 mangoes
2 tangerines
2 passion fruits
5 tablespoons (75 ml) natural yogurt
8 tablespoons (120 ml) pineapple juice

Just when you thought mangoes couldn't get any better, in jumps passion fruit,
and both are offset by the citrusy tangerines.

**NUTRIENTS**

Beta-carotene, folic acid, vitamins B3,
C and E; calcium, iron, magnesium,
phosphorus, potassium, sodium,
sulphur, zinc; protein

| | |
|---|---|
| ENERGY | ★★★★☆ |
| DETOX | ★☆☆☆☆ |
| IMMUNITY | ★★★★☆ |
| DIGESTION | ★★☆☆☆ |
| SKIN | ★★★☆☆ |

# 301 | pink melon

2 handfuls strawberries
$\frac{1}{2}$ melon
5 tablespoons (75 ml) natural yogurt
6 tablespoons (90 ml) apple juice

Even though I don't normally like melon
with yogurt, this blend is fantastic.

**NUTRIENTS**

Beta-carotene, biotin, folic acid,
vitamin C; calcium, magnesium,
phosphorus, potassium, sodium,
sulphur; protein

| | |
|---|---|
| ENERGY | ★★★★☆ |
| DETOX | ★☆☆☆☆ |
| IMMUNITY | ★★★★☆ |
| DIGESTION | ★★★☆☆ |
| SKIN | ★★★★☆ |

# 302 | pure pink thickie

2 handfuls strawberries
3 handfuls raspberries
5 tablespoons (75 ml) natural yogurt
6 tablespoons (90 ml) mineral water

Everybody's summer favourites in a thick, creamy drink. Berries lend
themselves perfectly to creamy smoothies.

**NUTRIENTS**

Beta-carotene, biotin, folic acid,
vitamin C; calcium, magnesium,
manganese, phosphorus, potassium,
sodium, sulphur; protein

| | |
|---|---|
| ENERGY | ★★★★☆ |
| DETOX | ★☆☆☆☆ |
| IMMUNITY | ★★★★☆ |
| DIGESTION | ★★☆☆☆ |
| SKIN | ★★★★☆ |

## 303 | creamy pink banana II

1 handful strawberries
1 handful raspberries
1 banana
5 tablespoons (75 ml) natural yogurt
6 tablespoons (90 ml) apple juice

Pink berry treats with another firm favourite.

### NUTRIENTS

Beta-carotene, biotin, folic acid,
vitamins B1, B3, B6 and C; calcium,
magnesium, manganese, phosphorus,
potassium, sodium, sulphur; protein

| | |
|---|---|
| ENERGY | ★★★★☆ |
| DETOX | ★☆☆☆☆ |
| IMMUNITY | ★★★★☆ |
| DIGESTION | ★★★☆☆ |
| SKIN | ★★★☆☆ |

## 304 | tropical pinkie

1 handful strawberries
1 handful raspberries
$\frac{1}{2}$ pineapple
5 tablespoons (75 ml) natural yogurt
6 tablespoons (90 ml) pineapple juice

Pineapple crushes up fantastically with these succulent berries.

### NUTRIENTS

Beta-carotene, biotin, folic acid,
vitamin C; calcium, magnesium,
manganese, phosphorus, potassium,
sodium, sulphur; protein

| | |
|---|---|
| ENERGY | ★★★★☆ |
| DETOX | ★☆☆☆☆ |
| IMMUNITY | ★★★★☆ |
| DIGESTION | ★★★☆☆ |
| SKIN | ★★★☆☆ |

## 305 | creamy berry tang

2 handfuls raspberries
2 oranges
5 tablespoons (75 ml) natural yogurt
6 tablespoons (90 ml) guava juice

The guava juice really brings out the flavours in this one.

### NUTRIENTS

Beta-carotene, biotin, folic acid,
vitamin B3, vitamin C; calcium,
magnesium, manganese, phosphorus,
potassium, sodium, sulphur; protein

| | |
|---|---|
| ENERGY | ★★★★☆ |
| DETOX | ★☆☆☆☆ |
| IMMUNITY | ★★★★☆ |
| DIGESTION | ★★☆☆☆ |
| SKIN | ★★★★☆ |

# 306 | purple rain

1 handful blueberries
1 handful blackberries
1 handful blackcurrants
5 tablespoons (75 ml) natural yogurt
6 tablespoons (90 ml) apple juice

Get them all in, any black or blue you can get your hands on, for a powerful taste sensation, not to mention a glassful of goodness.

**NUTRIENTS**

Beta-carotene, biotin, folic acid, vitamins B1, B2, B5, B6, C and E; calcium, chromium, iron, magnesium, manganese, phosphorus, potassium, sodium, sulphur, zinc; protein

| | |
|---|---|
| ENERGY | ★★★★☆ |
| DETOX | ★☆☆☆☆ |
| IMMUNITY | ★★★★☆ |
| DIGESTION | ★★★☆☆ |
| SKIN | ★★★★☆ |

# 307 | mighty berry

4 handfuls blueberries, blackberries, blackcurrants, strawberries, raspberries
5 tablespoons (75 ml) natural yogurt
6 tablespoons (90 ml) cranberry juice

Purple Rain plus the red ones too – a serious berry bonanza in a creamy base.

**NUTRIENTS**

Beta-carotene, biotin, folic acid, vitamins B1, B2, B5, B6, C and E; calcium, chromium, iron, magnesium, manganese, phosphorus, potassium, sodium, sulphur, zinc; protein

| | |
|---|---|
| ENERGY | ★★★★☆ |
| DETOX | ★★☆☆☆ |
| IMMUNITY | ★★★★☆ |
| DIGESTION | ★★★☆☆ |
| SKIN | ★★★★☆ |

# 308 | purple 'nana

3 handfuls blueberries, blackberries, blackcurrants
1 banana
5 tablespoons (75 ml) natural yogurt
6 tablespoons (90 ml) apple juice

Purple Rain with that smoothie favourite fruit – banana.

**NUTRIENTS**

Beta-carotene, biotin, folic acid, vitamins B1, B2, B5, B6, C and E; calcium, chromium, iron, magnesium, manganese, phosphorus, potassium, sodium, sulphur, zinc; protein

| | |
|---|---|
| ENERGY | ★★★★☆ |
| DETOX | ★☆☆☆☆ |
| IMMUNITY | ★★★★☆ |
| DIGESTION | ★★★☆☆ |
| SKIN | ★★★★☆ |

# 309 | mango in disguise

3 handfuls blueberries and blackberries
1 mango (or 2!)
5 tablespoons (75 ml) natural yogurt
6 tablespoons (90 ml) guava juice

You can barely discern the mango from the colour, but its taste certainly reminds you it's there, and the guava adds a different dimension altogether.

## NUTRIENTS

Beta-carotene, biotin, folic acid, vitamins B1, B2, B6, C and E; calcium, chromium, iron, magnesium, manganese, phosphorus, potassium, sodium, sulphur, zinc; protein

| | |
|---|---|
| ENERGY | ★★★★☆ |
| DETOX | ★☆☆☆☆ |
| IMMUNITY | ★★★★☆ |
| DIGESTION | ★★★☆☆ |
| SKIN | ★★★★☆ |

# 310 | purple pineapple

3 handfuls blueberries, blackberries, blackcurrants
$\frac{1}{2}$ pineapple
5 tablespoons (75 ml) natural yogurt
6 tablespoons (90 ml) pineapple juice

The tangy, tropical taste of pineapple blends beautifully with the berries. You could even use canned fruits in the winter.

## NUTRIENTS

Beta-carotene, biotin, folic acid, vitamins B1, B2, B6, C and E; calcium, chromium, iron, magnesium, manganese, phosphorus, potassium, sodium, sulphur, zinc; protein

| | |
|---|---|
| ENERGY | ★★★★☆ |
| DETOX | ★☆☆☆☆ |
| IMMUNITY | ★★★★☆ |
| DIGESTION | ★★★☆☆ |
| SKIN | ★★★★☆ |

## 311 | passionate pine

½ pineapple
½ banana
2 passion fruit
5 tablespoons (75 ml) natural yogurt
8 tablespoons (120 ml) pineapple juice

Almost anything with passion fruit is a hit
for me and this is definitely no exception.

### NUTRIENTS

Beta-carotene, folic acid, vitamins B1, B3,
B6 and C; calcium, magnesium, manganese,
phosphorus, potassium, sodium, sulphur,
zinc; protein

| | |
|---|---|
| ENERGY | ★★★★☆ |
| DETOX | ★☆☆☆☆ |
| IMMUNITY | ★★☆☆☆ |
| DIGESTION | ★★★★☆ |
| SKIN | ★☆☆☆☆ |

## 312 | pure pineapple creamy

½ pineapple
5 tablespoons (75 ml) natural yogurt
8 tablespoons (120 ml) pineapple juice

Sometimes the simple ones are the best. Pick a perfectly ripe pineapple
to get the optimum result.

### NUTRIENTS

Beta-carotene, folic acid, vitamin C;
calcium, magnesium, manganese,
phosphorus, potassium, sodium,
zinc; protein

| | |
|---|---|
| ENERGY | ★★★★☆ |
| DETOX | ★☆☆☆☆ |
| IMMUNITY | ★★★☆☆ |
| DIGESTION | ★★★★☆ |
| SKIN | ★★☆☆☆ |

# 313 | pina banana

$\frac{1}{2}$ pineapple
2 bananas
2 tablespoons (30 ml) coconut milk
5 tablespoons (75 ml) natural yogurt
6 tablespoons (90 ml) pineapple juice

A truly tropical taste.

## NUTRIENTS

Beta-carotene, folic acid, vitamins B1,
B3, B5, B6, C and E; calcium, magnesium,
manganese, phosphorus, potassium,
sodium, sulphur, zinc; protein

| | |
|---|---|
| ENERGY | ★★★★☆ |
| DETOX | ★☆☆☆☆ |
| IMMUNITY | ★★★☆☆ |
| DIGESTION | ★★★☆☆ |
| SKIN | ★☆☆☆☆ |

# 314 | creamy blue pine

$\frac{1}{2}$ pineapple
2 handfuls blueberries
5 tablespoons (75 ml) natural yogurt
8 tablespoons (120 ml) pineapple juice

There's something about the delicious but gentle taste of blueberries
that matches perfectly with tangy pineapple.

## NUTRIENTS

Beta-carotene, biotin, folic acid,
vitamins B1, B2, B6, C and E; calcium,
chromium, magnesium, manganese,
phosphorus, potassium, sodium,
zinc; protein

| | |
|---|---|
| ENERGY | ★★★★☆ |
| DETOX | ★☆☆☆☆ |
| IMMUNITY | ★★★★☆ |
| DIGESTION | ★★★★☆ |
| SKIN | ★★★★☆ |

# 315 | pinkypine

$\frac{1}{2}$ pineapple
1 handful strawberries
5 tablespoons (75 ml) natural yogurt
8 tablespoons (120 ml) guava juice

As if the fruit combination wasn't enough to make you salivate,
the guava on top...

## NUTRIENTS

Beta-carotene, biotin, folic acid,
vitamin B3, vitamin C; calcium,
magnesium, manganese, phosphorus,
potassium, sodium, sulphur, zinc;
protein

| | |
|---|---|
| ENERGY | ★★★★☆ |
| DETOX | ★☆☆☆☆ |
| IMMUNITY | ★★★★☆ |
| DIGESTION | ★★★☆☆ |
| SKIN | ★★★★☆ |

## 316 | pure peachy cream

4 peaches
5 tablespoons (75 ml) natural yogurt
8 tablespoons (120 ml) mineral water

Some would ask, why adulterate them with any other fruit?

### NUTRIENTS

Beta-carotene, folic acid,
vitamin B3, vitamin C; calcium,
magnesium, phosphorus, potassium,
sodium, sulphur, zinc; protein

| | |
|---|---|
| ENERGY | ★★★★☆ |
| DETOX | ★☆☆☆☆ |
| IMMUNITY | ★★★★☆ |
| DIGESTION | ★★★☆☆ |
| SKIN | ★★★☆☆ |

## 317 | vanilla peach

3 peaches
1 banana
$\frac{1}{2}$ teaspoon vanilla essence
5 tablespoons (75 ml) natural yogurt
8 tablespoons (120 ml) pineapple juice

They're good alone, but most fruits blend well with a banana, the ultimate smoothie fruit.

### NUTRIENTS

Beta-carotene, folic acid, vitamins B1,
B3, B6 and C; calcium, magnesium,
phosphorus, potassium, sodium,
sulphur, zinc; protein

| | |
|---|---|
| ENERGY | ★★★★☆ |
| DETOX | ★☆☆☆☆ |
| IMMUNITY | ★★★☆☆ |
| DIGESTION | ★★★★☆ |
| SKIN | ★★☆☆☆ |

## 318 | peachy passion

2 peaches
$\frac{1}{4}$ pineapple
2 passion fruits
5 tablespoons (75 ml) natural yogurt
8 tablespoons (120 ml) pineapple juice

Another tropical and temperate blend that turns out perfectly.

### NUTRIENTS

Beta-carotene, folic acid, vitamin B3,
vitamin C; calcium, iron, magnesium,
manganese, phosphorus, potassium,
sodium, sulphur, zinc; protein

| | |
|---|---|
| ENERGY | ★★★★☆ |
| DETOX | ★☆☆☆☆ |
| IMMUNITY | ★★★☆☆ |
| DIGESTION | ★★★☆☆ |
| SKIN | ★★★☆☆ |

## 319 | colour blend

2 peaches
1 banana
1 handful raspberries
5 tablespoons (75 ml) natural yogurt
8 tablespoons (120 ml) pineapple juice

Yellow and red make orange – here we have all three. Best made in the summer with juicy, ripe peaches and raspberries.

**NUTRIENTS**

Beta-carotene, biotin, folic acid, vitamins B1, B3, B6 and C; calcium, magnesium, phosphorus, potassium, sodium, sulphur, zinc; protein

| | |
|---|---|
| ENERGY | ★★★★☆ |
| DETOX | ★☆☆☆☆ |
| IMMUNITY | ★★★☆☆ |
| DIGESTION | ★★☆☆☆ |
| SKIN | ★★★☆☆ |

## 320 | apricot regular

8 rehydrated dried apricots
5 rehydrated prunes
5 tablespoons (75 ml) natural yogurt
8 tablespoons (120 ml) prune juice

Of course you can use any dried fruit, but this one's particularly good and extremely rich in fibre and antioxidants. It's best to soak the fruit overnight before blending it.

**NUTRIENTS**

Beta-carotene, folic acid, vitamins B3, B5 and C; calcium, magnesium, phosphorus, potassium, sodium, sulphur, zinc; protein

| | |
|---|---|
| ENERGY | ★★★★☆ |
| DETOX | ★☆☆☆☆ |
| IMMUNITY | ★★★★☆ |
| DIGESTION | ★★★★☆ |
| SKIN | ★★★★☆ |

# making
# quenchers
## chapter 4

As if all the other recipes in this book weren't refreshing enough, with quenchers we take that concept to another level. The drinks in this section are largely made with frozen fruit and ice; even the warm teas have a sensationally refreshing taste and texture.

We start with the frozen-fruit quenchers, drinks made by mixing frozen fruit pieces with juices, water, sorbets and ice in a blender to produce delicious combinations, all icy-cold on the palate. Next, the fizzy quenchers are great summer coolers, made by simply mixing all the ingredients (including sparkling mineral water) together in a jug. Finally, the tea-based recipes include home-made blends of warming spices, as well as a selection of cold teas to stimulate and revive the mind and spirit.

Guidelines for making the fizzy and tea-based quenchers are given with each recipe. All of the recipes make two generous portions.

# top tips

Below are a few reminders and helpful hints, tips and suggestions to enable you to get the most from making your quenchers.

1    To make frozen-fruit quenchers, drop all of the ingredients into a blender and mix them together for about a minute.

2    To make fizzy quenchers, stir all of the ingredients (including juiced or blended fruit where indicated) together in a large jug.

3    Add some pieces of chopped fruit to your fizzy quenchers to make them more like a summer cocktail.

4    If you want to make a frozen-fruit quencher but are out of frozen fruit, a time-saving alternative is to cheat by using fresh fruit blended with ice.

5    You can make bags of frozen fruit in advance – just prepare the fruit as you would for a smoothie then chop into pieces and divide into convenient sized portions in freezer bags and put in the freezer.

6    To freeze bananas, simply peel them and put them into a freezer bag whole – there is no need to chop them up.

7    When a recipe lists a particular sorbet as one of the ingredients, consider this a suggestion only. Use any sorbet you may have in the freezer – the chances are it'll be delicious whatever you try.

8    Once you've made a few of the recipes, play with the different blends, changing the ingredients to suit your tastes and the contents of your refrigerator, freezer or fruit bowl.

9    With the hot, brewed teas such as Ginger Brew and Full Spice, you can leave the pan on the stove and heat it up later in the day, adding a bit more water and a few more spices. This will deepen the taste and produce a lovely, rich flavour.

10    Most herbs and spices make delicious teas that are also laden with health properties, so try using whatever you've got growing in the garden (or window box), as you're likely to be able to turn it into a refreshing, healthy tea.

# 321 | tangy banana freeze

2 frozen bananas
1 passion fruit
2 scoops lime sorbet
a few dashes of mineral water

Just blend all of these together for a fresh taste-bomb.

## NUTRIENTS

Beta-carotene, folic acid, vitamin B1, B3,
B6 and C; calcium, magnesium, phosphorus,
potassium, sodium, sulphur

| | |
|---|---|
| ENERGY | ★★★★★ |
| DETOX | ★☆☆☆☆ |
| IMMUNITY | ★★☆☆☆ |
| DIGESTION | ★★★☆☆ |
| SKIN | ★★★☆☆ |

# 322 | orange dream

2 oranges, juiced
4 nectarines
6 ice cubes

This one is like a sweet orange popsicle (ice-lolly) but even better thanks
to the nectarines.

## NUTRIENTS

Beta-carotene, folic acid, vitamin C;
calcium, magnesium, phosphorus,
potassium

| | |
|---|---|
| ENERGY | ★★★★★ |
| DETOX | ★★☆☆☆ |
| IMMUNITY | ★★★★★ |
| DIGESTION | ★☆☆☆☆ |
| SKIN | ★★★★☆ |

# 323 | lift off

2 grapefruits, juiced
$\frac{1}{2}$ pineapple
$\frac{1}{4}$ inch (0.5 cm) grated ginger root
6 ice cubes

This combination is a highly charged challenge to your tastebuds.

## NUTRIENTS

Beta-carotene, folic acid, vitamin C;
calcium, magnesium, manganese,
phosphorus, potassium, sodium,
sulphur

| | |
|---|---|
| ENERGY | ★★★★★ |
| DETOX | ★☆☆☆☆ |
| IMMUNITY | ★★★☆☆ |
| DIGESTION | ★★★☆☆ |
| SKIN | ★★★☆☆ |

## 324 | paw paw sharp

$\frac{1}{2}$ papaya
2 scoops lime sorbet
a few dashes of mineral water

I just love the Australian version of papaya – paw paw – and this drink certainly does it justice.

**NUTRIENTS**

Beta-carotene, folic acid, vitamin C;
calcium, magnesium, phosphorus,
potassium, sodium, sulphur

| | |
|---|---|
| ENERGY | ★★★★★ |
| DETOX | ★☆☆☆☆ |
| IMMUNITY | ★★★★☆ |
| DIGESTION | ★★★★☆ |
| SKIN | ★★★☆☆ |

## 325 | mango squeeze

2 grapefruits, juiced
2 mangoes
6 ice cubes

Mango is perfect for toning down the tanginess of the grapefruit – all in all super refreshing and a sweet but uplifting blend.

**NUTRIENTS**

Beta-carotene, folic acid, vitamin C,
vitamin E; calcium, iron, magnesium,
phosphorus, potassium, sodium, sulphur

| | |
|---|---|
| ENERGY | ★★★★★ |
| DETOX | ★☆☆☆☆ |
| IMMUNITY | ★★★★★ |
| DIGESTION | ★★☆☆☆ |
| SKIN | ★★★★☆ |

# 326 | pure pine freeze

$\frac{1}{2}$ pineapple, frozen in chunks
1 scoop lime sorbet
a few dashes of pineapple juice

It is hard to imagine anything more thirst quenching than this refreshing drink.

### NUTRIENTS

Beta-carotene, folic acid, vitamin C;
calcium, magnesium, manganese,
phosphorus, potassium, sodium,
sulphur

| | |
|---|---|
| ENERGY | ★★★★★ |
| DETOX | ★☆☆☆☆ |
| IMMUNITY | ★★☆☆☆ |
| DIGESTION | ★★★★☆ |
| SKIN | ★★★☆☆ |

# 327 | pine passion

$\frac{1}{2}$ pineapple, frozen in chunks
2 passion fruits
2 tablespoons (30 ml) natural yogurt
a few dashes of pineapple juice

In my view, you can barely go wrong with passion fruit, and blended with frozen, ripe pineapple … mmm.

### NUTRIENTS

Beta-carotene, folic acid, vitamins B3,
B12 and C; calcium, iron, magnesium,
manganese, phosphorus, potassium,
sodium, sulphur, zinc; protein

| | |
|---|---|
| ENERGY | ★★★★☆ |
| DETOX | ★☆☆☆☆ |
| IMMUNITY | ★★★☆☆ |
| DIGESTION | ★★★★☆ |
| SKIN | ★★★☆☆ |

# 328 | tropics at zero

$\frac{1}{2}$ pineapple, frozen in chunks
1 mango, frozen in chunks
1 scoop lime sorbet
a few dashes of pineapple juice

You'd certainly need this one on a hot beach in the tropics.

### NUTRIENTS

Beta-carotene, folic acid, vitamin C,
vitamin E; calcium, iron, magnesium,
manganese, phosphorus, potassium,
sodium, sulphur

| | |
|---|---|
| ENERGY | ★★★★★ |
| DETOX | ★☆☆☆☆ |
| IMMUNITY | ★★★★☆ |
| DIGESTION | ★★★☆☆ |
| SKIN | ★★★★☆ |

## 329 | strawberries on sunbeds

½ pineapple, frozen in chunks
1 handful frozen strawberries
1 tablespoon (15 ml) coconut milk
a few dashes of pineapple juice

Sit back and relax – you'd be forgiven for wondering where in the world
you are with this sublime mix.

**NUTRIENTS**

Beta-carotene, biotin, folic acid,
vitamin C; calcium, magnesium,
manganese, phosphorus, potassium,
sodium, sulphur

| | |
|---|---|
| ENERGY | ★★★★★ |
| DETOX | ★☆☆☆☆ |
| IMMUNITY | ★★★★☆ |
| DIGESTION | ★★☆☆☆ |
| SKIN | ★★★☆☆ |

## 330 | malibu freeze

½ pineapple, frozen in chunks
1 banana, frozen
1 tablespoon (15 ml) coconut milk
½ lime, juiced
a few dashes of pineapple juice

Transport yourself to beneath a palm tree with this creamy cooler.

**NUTRIENTS**

Beta-carotene, folic acid, vitamins B1,
B3, B6 and C; calcium, magnesium,
manganese, phosphorus, potassium,
sodium, sulphur

| | |
|---|---|
| ENERGY | ★★★★★ |
| DETOX | ★☆☆☆☆ |
| IMMUNITY | ★★☆☆☆ |
| DIGESTION | ★★★☆☆ |
| SKIN | ★★★☆☆ |

# 331 | pink banana freeze

2 handfuls frozen strawberries
2 frozen bananas
a few dashes orange juice

A classic smoothie, with a frozen touch.

### NUTRIENTS

| | | |
|---|---|---|
| Beta-carotene, folic acid, biotin, | ENERGY | ★★★★★ |
| vitamins B1, B3, B6 and C; calcium, | DETOX | ★☆☆☆☆ |
| magnesium, phosphorus, potassium, | IMMUNITY | ★★★☆☆ |
| sulphur | DIGESTION | ★★☆☆☆ |
| | SKIN | ★★★☆☆ |

# 332 | double red

4 handfuls frozen raspberries
a few dashes cranberry juice

Tangy and sweet all at once, this bright red freezie is exquisite.

### NUTRIENTS

| | | |
|---|---|---|
| Beta-carotene, biotin, folic acid, vitamin C; | ENERGY | ★★★★☆ |
| calcium, iron, magnesium, manganese, | DETOX | ★☆☆☆☆ |
| phosphorus, potassium, sodium, sulphur | IMMUNITY | ★★★☆☆ |
| | DIGESTION | ☆☆☆☆☆ |
| | SKIN | ★★★☆☆ |

# 333 | double red creamy

2 handfuls frozen raspberries
2 handfuls frozen strawberries
2 tablespoons (30 ml) natural yogurt
a few dashes cranberry juice

A sweeter, creamier version of Double Red, made nice and thick with the addition of yogurt.

### NUTRIENTS

| | | |
|---|---|---|
| Beta-carotene, biotin, folic acid, | ENERGY | ★★★★☆ |
| vitamin B12, vitamin C; calcium, iron, | DETOX | ★☆☆☆☆ |
| magnesium, manganese, phosphorus, | IMMUNITY | ★★★☆☆ |
| potassium, sodium, sulphur, zinc, | DIGESTION | ★★☆☆☆ |
| | SKIN | ★★★☆☆ |

## 334 | peachy pink cream

2 handfuls frozen strawberries
2 peaches, frozen in chunks
2 tablespoons (30 ml) natural yogurt
a few dashes orange juice

An idyllic combination with a creamy touch.

**NUTRIENTS**

Beta-carotene, biotin, folic acid,
vitamins B3, B12 and C; calcium,
magnesium, phosphorus, potassium,
sodium, sulphur, zinc; protein

| | |
|---|---|
| ENERGY | ★★★★☆ |
| DETOX | ★☆☆☆☆ |
| IMMUNITY | ★★★★☆ |
| DIGESTION | ★★☆☆☆ |
| SKIN | ★★★☆☆ |

## 335 | big black freeze

4 handfuls frozen blueberries, blackberries, blackcurrants
2 tablespoons (30 ml) natural yogurt
a few dashes apple juice

Whatever the weather, you'd almost believe it was summer when sipping this cooling refresher.

**NUTRIENTS**

Beta-carotene, biotin, folic acid,
vitamins B1, B2, B6, B12, C and, E;
calcium, chromium, magnesium,
manganese, phosphorus, potassium,
sodium, sulphur, zinc; protein

| | |
|---|---|
| ENERGY | ★★★★☆ |
| DETOX | ★☆☆☆☆ |
| IMMUNITY | ★★★★★ |
| DIGESTION | ★★★☆☆ |
| SKIN | ★★★★☆ |

## 336 | black & apple freezie

4 handfuls frozen blackberries
2 tablespoons (30 ml) natural yogurt
$\frac{1}{2}$ teaspoon vanilla essence
a few dashes apple juice

That classic English combination with a smooth vanilla undertone.

**NUTRIENTS**

Beta-carotene, folic acid, vitamin C,
vitamin E; calcium, iron, magnesium,
manganese, phosphorus, potassium,
sodium, sulphur; protein

| | |
|---|---|
| ENERGY | ★★★★☆ |
| DETOX | ★☆☆☆☆ |
| IMMUNITY | ★★☆☆☆ |
| DIGESTION | ☆☆☆☆☆ |
| SKIN | ★★★☆☆ |

## 337 | creamy apple freezie

4 tablespoons (60 ml) frozen stewed apple
1 fresh apple, cored, chopped and peeled
4 tablespoons (60 ml) natural yogurt
$\frac{1}{4}$ teaspoon ground cinnamon
$\frac{1}{2}$ teaspoon vanilla essence
a few dashes apple juice

This combination is especially good if you've used a sharp variety
of apple such as Granny Smith.

| NUTRIENTS | | |
|---|---|---|
| Beta-carotene, folic acid, vitamin B12, | ENERGY | ★★★★☆ |
| vitamin C; calcium, magnesium, phosphorus, | DETOX | ★☆☆☆☆ |
| potassium, sulphur, zinc; protein | IMMUNITY | ★★★☆☆ |
| | DIGESTION | ★★★★☆ |
| | SKIN | ★★☆☆☆ |

## 338 | gingapple

4 tablespoons (60 ml) frozen stewed apple
2 fresh apples, cored, chopped and peeled
$\frac{1}{4}$ inch (0.5 cm) fresh ginger root, grated
2 scoops lime sorbet
a few dashes apple juice

A deliciously refreshing combination with a sharp bite from the
ginger and lime.

| NUTRIENTS | | |
|---|---|---|
| Beta-carotene, folic acid, vitamin C; | ENERGY | ★★★★☆ |
| calcium, magnesium, phosphorus, | DETOX | ★☆☆☆☆ |
| potassium, sodium, sulphur | IMMUNITY | ★★★☆☆ |
| | DIGESTION | ★★★☆☆ |
| | SKIN | ★★☆☆☆ |

## 339 | pine apple

4 tablespoons (60 ml) frozen stewed apple
$\frac{1}{2}$ pineapple, frozen in chunks
2 scoops lime sorbet
a few dashes apple juice

A wonderfully fresh blend of fruits, given a sweet tang by the
lime sorbet.

| NUTRIENTS | | |
|---|---|---|
| Beta-carotene, folic acid, vitamin C; | ENERGY | ★★★★☆ |
| calcium, magnesium, manganese, | DETOX | ★☆☆☆☆ |
| phosphorus, potassium, sodium, sulphur | IMMUNITY | ★★☆☆☆ |
| | DIGESTION | ★★★☆☆ |
| | SKIN | ★★☆☆☆ |

## 340 | apple & prune freeze

4 tablespoons (60 ml) frozen stewed apple
8 rehydrated prunes
½ teaspoon vanilla essence
4 tablespoons (60 ml) natural yogurt
a few dashes apple juice

This one is so creamy and sweet – a full meal in itself.

**NUTRIENTS**

Beta-carotene, folic acid, vitamin B12,
vitamin C; calcium, magnesium, phosphorus,
potassium, sulphur, zinc; protein

| | |
|---|---|
| ENERGY | ★★★★☆ |
| DETOX | ★☆☆☆☆ |
| IMMUNITY | ★★★★☆ |
| DIGESTION | ★★★★☆ |
| SKIN | ★★☆☆☆ |

## 341 | blue apple

4 tablespoons (60 ml) frozen stewed apple
2 handfuls frozen blueberries
2 tablespoons (30 ml) natural yogurt
a few dashes apple juice

The flecks of blue from the blueberry skins let you in on the secret
of how delicious this creamy frozen-fruit quencher really is.

**NUTRIENTS**

Beta-carotene, folic acid, vitamin B12,
vitamin C; calcium, chromium, magnesium,
phosphorus, potassium, sodium, sulphur,
zinc; protein

| | |
|---|---|
| ENERGY | ★★★★☆ |
| DETOX | ★☆☆☆☆ |
| IMMUNITY | ★★★★☆ |
| DIGESTION | ★★★☆☆ |
| SKIN | ★★★★☆ |

# 342 | watermelon tanger

½ watermelon
2 scoops lime sorbet
6 ice cubes

Watermelon is one of the most refreshing fruits, at 95% water, and with the lime added, it's even better. Ideal for a baking hot day.

**NUTRIENTS**

Beta-carotene, folic acid, vitamin B5,
vitamin C; calcium, magnesium, phosphorus,
potassium, sodium, sulphur

| | |
|---|---|
| ENERGY | ★★★★★ |
| DETOX | ★☆☆☆☆ |
| IMMUNITY | ★★★★☆ |
| DIGESTION | ☆☆☆☆☆ |
| SKIN | ★★★★☆ |

# 343 | pink ice

½ watermelon
2 handfuls frozen strawberries
1 scoop lemon sorbet
6 ice cubes
a few dashes of mineral water

Just by looking at this vision in pink, you'll know it's delicious and good for you.

**NUTRIENTS**

Beta-carotene, biotin, folic acid,
vitamin B5, vitamin C; calcium,
magnesium, phosphorus, potassium,
sodium, sulphur

| | |
|---|---|
| ENERGY | ★★★★★ |
| DETOX | ★☆☆☆☆ |
| IMMUNITY | ★★★★☆ |
| DIGESTION | ★☆☆☆☆ |
| SKIN | ★★★★☆ |

# 344 | peachy mango ice

1 mango, frozen in chunks
3 peaches, frozen in chunks
a few dashes of orange juice

Double trouble from two delicious orange fruits that blend beautifully, especially in a frosty drink.

**NUTRIENTS**

Beta-carotene, folic acid, vitamins B3,
C and E; calcium, iron, magnesium,
phosphorus, potassium, sodium,
sulphur

| | |
|---|---|
| ENERGY | ★★★★★ |
| DETOX | ★★☆☆☆ |
| IMMUNITY | ★★★★★ |
| DIGESTION | ★★☆☆☆ |
| SKIN | ★★★★★ |

## 345 | mango surprise

2 mangoes, frozen in chunks
juice of one lime
$\frac{1}{2}$ inch (1 cm) grated ginger root
4 tablespoons (60 ml) natural yogurt
6 ice cubes

Your tastebuds won't know what hit them – smooth mango, sharp lime, zingy ginger and creamy yogurt create a winning combination.

**NUTRIENTS**

Beta-carotene, folic acid, vitamins B12,
C and E; calcium, iron, magnesium,
phosphorus, potassium, sodium,
sulphur, zinc; protein

| | |
|---|---|
| ENERGY | ★★★★☆ |
| DETOX | ★☆☆☆☆ |
| IMMUNITY | ★★★☆☆ |
| DIGESTION | ★★★☆☆ |
| SKIN | ★★★☆☆ |

## 346 | apricot banana ice

2 frozen bananas
6 frozen apricots
a few dashes of apple juice

You have to freeze well-ripened apricots to bring out the taste in this sumptuous quencher; otherwise, freeze apricots that have been canned in juice.

**NUTRIENTS**

Beta-carotene, folic acid, vitamins B1,
B3, B5, B6 and C; calcium, magnesium,
phosphorus, potassium, sulphur

| | |
|---|---|
| ENERGY | ★★★★★ |
| DETOX | ★☆☆☆☆ |
| IMMUNITY | ★★★☆☆ |
| DIGESTION | ★★☆☆☆ |
| SKIN | ★★★☆☆ |

## 347 | kiwi berry

3 kiwi fruits
2 handfuls frozen strawberries
a few dashes of apple juice
4–6 ice cubes

Grab a high dose of vitamin C in this delicious combination.

**NUTRIENTS**

Beta-carotene, biotin, folic acid,
vitamin C; calcium, magnesium, phosphorus,
potassium, sodium, sulphur

| | |
|---|---|
| ENERGY | ★★★★★ |
| DETOX | ★★★☆☆ |
| IMMUNITY | ★★★★★ |
| DIGESTION | ★★☆☆☆ |
| SKIN | ★★★★★ |

# 348 | lime cooler

juice of three limes
1 pt (500 ml) sparkling mineral water
4–6 fresh mint leaves
4–6 ice cubes

A classic, cooling summer drink, perfect in its simplicity.

**NUTRIENTS**

Beta-carotene, folic acid, vitamin C;
calcium, magnesium, phosphorus,
potassium, sodium, sulphur

| | |
|---|---|
| ENERGY | ★☆☆☆☆ |
| DETOX | ★★☆☆☆ |
| IMMUNITY | ★★★☆☆ |
| DIGESTION | ★☆☆☆☆ |
| SKIN | ★★☆☆☆ |

# 349 | orange passion twinkle

4 oranges, juiced
4 passion fruits
sparkling mineral water to top up
4–6 ice cubes

Perfect on a hot summer's day, just stir in the passion fruit. If you don't like the seeds, pass them through a strainer first.

**NUTRIENTS**

Beta-carotene, vitamin B3, vitamin C;
calcium, magnesium, phosphorus,
potassium, sodium

| | |
|---|---|
| ENERGY | ★★★★☆ |
| DETOX | ★★☆☆☆ |
| IMMUNITY | ★★★★☆ |
| DIGESTION | ☆☆☆☆☆ |
| SKIN | ★★☆☆☆ |

# 350 | grape cooler

2 grapefruits, juiced
1 scoop orange sorbet
$\frac{1}{4}$ inch (0.5 cm) grated ginger root
sparkling mineral water to top up
4–6 ice cubes

Just let the sorbet melt, sweeten and froth up the freshly squeezed juice before splashing in the mineral water to give it fizz.

**NUTRIENTS**

Beta-carotene, folic acid, vitamin C;
calcium, magnesium, phosphorus,
potassium, sulphur

| | |
|---|---|
| ENERGY | ★★★★☆ |
| DETOX | ★★☆☆☆ |
| IMMUNITY | ★★★★☆ |
| DIGESTION | ★☆☆☆☆ |
| SKIN | ★★☆☆☆ |

# 351 | pine fizz

$\frac{1}{2}$ pineapple, juiced
4–6 fresh mint leaves
sparkling mineral water to top up
4–6 ice cubes

Somehow, pineapples really suit being fizzy.

### NUTRIENTS

Beta-carotene, folic acid, vitamin C;
calcium, magnesium, manganese,
phosphorus, potassium, sodium

| | |
|---|---|
| ENERGY | ★★★★☆ |
| DETOX | ★★★☆☆ |
| IMMUNITY | ★★★☆☆ |
| DIGESTION | ★★★☆☆ |
| SKIN | ★★☆☆☆ |

# 352 | pick-me-up fizz

$\frac{1}{2}$ pineapple, juiced
2 oranges, juiced
sparkling mineral water to top up
4–6 ice cubes

Fresh, tangy, sharp, juicy, fizzy – all sensations to liven you up.

### NUTRIENTS

Beta-carotene, folic acid, vitamin C;
calcium, magnesium, manganese,
phosphorus, potassium, sodium

| | |
|---|---|
| ENERGY | ★★★★☆ |
| DETOX | ★★☆☆☆ |
| IMMUNITY | ★★★★☆ |
| DIGESTION | ★★☆☆☆ |
| SKIN | ★★★☆☆ |

# 353 | melon tang

1 melon
$\frac{1}{4}$ inch (0.5 cm) grated ginger root
juice of a lime
4–6 ice cubes
sparkling mineral water to top up

Blend the melon, lime juice, ginger and ice before topping up to a fizzy cooler.

### NUTRIENTS

Beta-carotene, folic acid, vitamin C;
calcium, magnesium, phosphorus,
potassium, sodium, sulphur

| | |
|---|---|
| ENERGY | ★★★★☆ |
| DETOX | ★★☆☆☆ |
| IMMUNITY | ★★★☆☆ |
| DIGESTION | ★★☆☆☆ |
| SKIN | ★★★☆☆ |

# 354 | fizzy berry crush

2 handfuls strawberries
2 handfuls blueberries
4–6 ice cubes
sparkling mineral water to top up

Instead of fruit juice, use fruit pulp by blending
the strawberries and blueberries with the ice, so
you get a fantastic texture as well as taste.

**NUTRIENTS**
Beta-carotene, biotin, folic acid,
vitamins B1, B2, B6, C and E; calcium,
chromium, magnesium, phosphorus,
potassium, sodium, sulphur

| | |
|---|---|
| ENERGY | ★★★★☆ |
| DETOX | ★★★☆☆ |
| IMMUNITY | ★★★★★ |
| DIGESTION | ☆☆☆☆☆ |
| SKIN | ★★★★☆ |

# 355 | kiwi melon

$\frac{1}{2}$ melon
2 kiwi fruits
juice of a lime
4–6 ice cubes
sparkling mineral water to top up

Another blended fizzie – pulp the melon, kiwi, lime juice and ice
before adding the mineral water for a delicious summery cocktail.

**NUTRIENTS**
Beta-carotene, folic acid, vitamin C;
calcium, magnesium, phosphorus,
potassium, sodium, sulphur

| | |
|---|---|
| ENERGY | ★★★★☆ |
| DETOX | ★★★☆☆ |
| IMMUNITY | ★★★★★ |
| DIGESTION | ★☆☆☆☆ |
| SKIN | ★★★★☆ |

## 356 | apple spice

$\frac{1}{4}$ inch (0.5 cm) ginger root, grated or finely sliced
2 cinnamon sticks
7 fl oz (200 ml) water
1 teaspoon honey
4 tablespoons frozen stewed apple
7 fl oz (200 ml) apple juice

This is a delicious blend of apples and spices in a summer drink. Alternatively, you could drink it warm on a cold winter's night.

Bring the water, ginger and cinnamon to the boil and leave to simmer for at least five minutes. Strain, add the honey and leave to cool. Meanwhile, mix the apple and apple juice in a blender and gradually add the cooled tea.

## 357 | fresh sensation

1 small bunch of fresh mint leaves
1 inch (2.5 cm) grated ginger root
9 fl oz (300 ml) water
4 oranges, freshly juiced
1 scoop lime sorbet
4–6 ice cubes

A combination of refreshing, tangy ingredients to cool down on a summer's day.

Pour boiling water over the leaves and grated ginger, steep for five minutes. Leave to cool, top up with freshly squeezed orange juice, lime sorbet and ice.

## 358 | ginger brew

1 inch (2.5 cm) grated ginger root
1 pt (500 ml) water

Neat ginger tea, refreshing and good for digestion.
If you find it a little strong-tasting, add a teaspoon
of honey for a more mellow flavour.

Bring to the boil and leave to simmer for at least five minutes.
Strain and serve.

## 359 | middle east ginger

1 inch (2.5 cm) grated ginger root
10 cardamom pods
1 pt (500 ml) water

Ginger Brew with a touch of the Middle East from the
cardamom, even better for digestion.

Bring to the boil and leave to simmer for at least five minutes.
Strain and serve.

## 360 | cold soother

2 sticks cinnamon
juice of a lemon
1 teaspoon honey
1 pt (500 ml) water

A warm drink to soothe the throat on a winter's day.

Bring water and cinnamon to the boil and leave to simmer for at
least five minutes. Strain, add the lemon juice and honey and serve.

## 361 | full spice

½ inch (1 cm) grated or finely sliced ginger root
4 cardamom pods
1 cinnamon stick
5 cloves
1 pt (500 ml) water

A complete blend of delicious spices for a warming
drink that's great for soothing the throat and digestion.

Bring to the boil and leave to simmer for at least five minutes.
Strain and serve.

## 362 | mint & honey

1 small bunch of fresh mint leaves
1 teaspoon honey
1 pt (500 ml) water

Fresh mint tea is probably the most refreshing hot drink there
is, and it's good for digestion. I don't usually add honey, but to
make it more like the sweet Middle Eastern version, you can stir
in a spoonful.

Pour boiling water over the leaves, steep for five minutes. If using honey, stir
it in and serve.

## 363 | tangy mint cooler

1 small bunch of fresh mint leaves
9 fl oz (300 ml) water
7 fl oz (200 ml) pineapple juice
4–6 ice cubes

A refreshing minty cocktail to stimulate the senses.

Make mint tea as in Mint & Honey (see above), leave to cool. Top up with
pineapple juice and add ice.

# 364 | rosehip rasp

1 rosehip teabag
14 fl oz (400 ml) water
1 handful raspberries
2 peaches, frozen in chunks
4–6 ice cubes

Rosehip tea has a sharp, fruity, refreshing taste –
the fruit contrasts with this perfectly and gives your
immune system an extra boost.

Pour boiling water over the teabag. Leave to steep and cool.
Meanwhile, blend the raspberries and peach. Stir the fruit pulp
into the cooled tea and add ice cubes.

# 365 | spicy peachy cream

4 cardamom pods
2 cinnamon sticks
7 fl oz (200 ml) water
3 peaches, frozen in chunks
$\frac{1}{2}$ teaspoon vanilla essence
3 tablespoons (45 ml) natural yogurt
3–5 ice cubes

This one is almost a dessert in itself – a
fantastic blend of eastern spices, fresh peaches
and creamy yogurt.

Bring the water, cardamom and cinnamon
to the boil and leave to simmer for at least
five minutes. Strain and leave to cool. Meanwhile
mix the peaches, vanilla and yogurt in blender
and gradually add the spice tea. Top with
ice cubes and sip slowly through a straw.

# juicing
# reference
## chapter 5

This section starts with four healthful programs to make choosing your juice recipes easy. If you're just getting into the habit, begin with The Basic Intro Week, to start you off gently on simple, delicious fruit and vegetable drinks. Then there's The Detox Week: juices chosen to accompany a basic detox program. If you tend to get every cough and cold going, you'd do well to give your immune system a boost by having a daily, fresh juice as suggested in The Immune Power Week. Finally, the last juice course is a wonderfully rejuvenating Juice High Weekend, where, for nearly 48 hours, you feast on nothing but juices.

Following on from the juice courses, you'll find two useful charts: a list of nutrients, what they're good for and rich food sources, then an easy reference of fruits, vegetables and juice recipes to help support you for a number of common ailments.

## the basic intro week

To inspire you through the maze of the countless combinations possible, this starter course introduces you to some juice recipes that are likely to become your staples. Working primarily with ingredients that you're most likely to have in your fruit bowl or refrigerator, we build up from simple fruit juices to blends you may initially have found a little challenging on the palate. Believe me, if you're not already, by the time you've got to the end of this week, you'll be a true juicing devotee.

| | |
|---|---|
| **Monday** | Sweet C Too (see p.31) |
| **Tuesday** | Pink Pear (see p.67) |
| **Wednesday** | Gently Raspberry (see p.58) |
| **Thursday** | Pineapple Basic (see p.73) |
| **Friday** | Orange Carrot (see p.78) |
| **Saturday** | Easy Morning (see p.77) |
| **Sunday** | Apple Cleanser (see p.33) |

## the detox week

Many health-conscious people occasionally "go on a detox". First, it's important to remember that our bodies are constantly detoxifying, not just when we choose. Second, some of the faddy programs are, in my view, too extreme and in some cases unhealthy. However, others programs encourage us to reassess what we are consuming, and leave us feeling rejuvenated, clearer in mind and body and bursting with energy. The recipes here are particularly cleansing blends aimed at supporting you during a sensible detox program.

| | |
|---|---|
| **Monday** | Apple Cleanser (see p.33) |
| **Tuesday** | Green Hit (see p.83) |
| **Wednesday** | Carrot Cleanser (see p.78) |
| **Thursday** | Beet Basic (see p.95) |
| **Friday** | Green Goddess (see p.91) |
| **Saturday** | Green 'n' Pear It (see p.91) |
| **Sunday** | Green Pines (see p.75) |

## the immune-power week

If you've noticed that your body's defences are not up to scratch – you pick up any passing cold and regularly suffer from throat or bladder infections – your immune system may need a hand. Even if you've always had a tendency to get ill, you should find that giving yourself a boost with fresh, raw juices and smoothies helps keep colds at bay, let alone anything more serious. These recipes are particularly powerful immune-boosters for a concerted one-week course, but you'll feel even more benefit if you make juicing an ongoing delight.

| | |
|---|---|
| **Monday** | Power Packed C (see p.49) |
| **Tuesday** | Carotene Kick (see p.97) |
| **Wednesday** | Cold War (see p.81) |
| **Thursday** | Grapefruit Blues (see p.42) |
| **Friday** | Greatfruit C (see p.42) |
| **Saturday** | Carotene Catapult (see p.80) |
| **Sunday** | Green Tomatoes (see p.100) |

## the juice high weekend

By consuming nothing but raw, fresh juices for a weekend, you give your body a break from the foods and drinks that normally travel through your insides. This way, the body has a chance to do a bit of its own housework and leave you rejuvenated and feeling like you're making a fresh start. It is also a good step in helping you kick a toxic habit such as smoking. This may not sound like a huge amount of fun, and it is likely to be challenging, so it's best to go on a juice fast over a weekend or two-day break, when you can relax and rest as you feel is necessary.

You'll find you get the most out of this course if you prepare yourself well beforehand by buying in all you need, and see it as treating yourself to two days of healthy calm. In addition to drinking the blends listed overleaf (about 6 glasses a day in total), I suggest you incorporate the following into your weekend: plenty of spring water, several snoozes (you may feel tired, irritable or get a bit of a headache), a sauna or steam, a warm bath (spinkle in a few drops of your favourite essential oils), a massage, gentle walks in fresh air, breathing exercises, and pastimes, such as reading, to keep you busy if you are not sleeping. Avoid strenuous exercise.

| **Day Before** | Eat light salads and fruit during the day. | |
| | Dinner | Green Hit (see p.83) |

| **Day One** | Breakfast | Apple Gone Loupey (see p.36) |
| | Late morning | Florida Blue (see p.48) |
| | Afternoon | Beetles (see p.95) |
| | Dinner | Green Goddess (see p.91) |

| **Day Two** | Breakfast | Carrot Deep Cleanser (see p.79) |
| | Mid-morning | Beet Basic (see p.95) |
| | Lunch | Large salad of fresh, raw vegetables and/or fruits. |
| | Dinner | Large salad of fresh, raw vegetables and/or fruits. |

It is crucial that you do not suddenly overload your body with large quantities of cooked or rich foods. Prepare a substantial, varied salad and dress it lightly with olive oil and lemon juice. Sit down to eat it and chew it well.

Most people are likely to feel a little tired doing the Juice High Weekend. You may also experience some bloating or flatulence, diarrhea, headaches, tiredness and sweating. These are normal; however, if they become excessive or you have other symptoms, you should visit a doctor. You should not undertake the Juice High Weekend if you are unwell, pregnant or on medication.

# nutrient chart

This chart lists the main nutrients that the body needs for optimum health. The right-hand column gives all the rich food sources for each nutrient – including foods that are not used in juices or smoothies but that should nevertheless form part of your regular diet.

| nutrient | benefits | rich food sources |
| --- | --- | --- |
| **vitamins** | | |
| **Vitamin A** | Important antioxidant, protects skin and keeps vision healthy; protects against cancer. | Butter, kidneys, liver, whole milk |
| **Beta-carotene** | Important antioxidant, protects skin – including "inside skins" such as the lining of intestines, lungs, nose and throat. Beta-carotene is the plant version of vitamin A. | Apricots, asparagus, broccoli, cantaloupe melon, carrots, kale, liver, pumpkin, spinach, sweet potato, watermelon |
| **Vitamin B1 (thiamine)** | Needed for energy production; and for the normal workings of the nervous system, muscles and heart, growth and development. | Beef kidney and liver, brewer's yeast, chickpeas, kidney beans, rice bran, salmon, soy (soya) beans, sunflower seeds, wheatgerm, whole grain wheat and rye |
| **Vitamin B2 (riboflavin)** | Needed for the production of energy from food, and for healthy skin and mucous membranes; needed for nerves to function well and for healthy growth and development. | Almonds, brewer's yeast, cheese, chicken, eggs, fish, milk, organic meats, wheatgerm, yogurt |
| **Vitamin B3 (niacin)** | Needed for the production of energy, the health of the nervous system, digestive system and skin; also needed to keep cholesterol levels low. | Beef liver, brewer's yeast, chicken, fish, nuts, potatoes, pulses, sunflower seeds, turkey |
| **Vitamin B5 (pantothenic acid)** | Needed for energy production, the body's response to stress, regeneration of all of cells, particularly in the nervous system, and antibodies. | Blue cheese, brewer's yeast, corn, dried fruit, eggs, lentils, liver, lobster, meat, nuts, peas, soy (soya) beans, sunflower seeds, wheatgerm, whole grain products, vegetables |
| **Vitamin B6 (pyridoxine)** | Needed for energy production, a healthy nervous system, brain and mental state, and for the body to build all types of cells, hormones and anti-bodies (defenders against infections). | Avocados, bananas, bran, brewer's yeast, carrots, eggs, hazelnuts, lean meat, lentils, rice, salmon, shrimps, soy (soya) beans, sunflower seeds, tuna, wheatgerm, wholewheat flour |
| **Vitamin B12 (cyanocobalamin)** | Particularly important for the health of the brain and nervous system and for formation of red blood cells. | Cheese, clams, eggs, fish, meat, milk and milk products, poultry. NB – vitamin B12 is not found in plant foods. |
| **Folic acid** | Needed for production of red blood cells, and the growth of healthy nerves, particularly in a developing fetus. | Barley, brewer's yeast, fruit, chickpeas, green leafy vegetables, lentils, liver, peas, rice, soy (soya) beans, wheatgerm |
| **Biotin** | Helps the body process sugars, carbohydrates, proteins and other vitamins; needed for healthy skin, nails and hair. | Brewer's yeast, brown rice, cashew nuts, cheese, chicken, eggs, lentils, liver, mackerel, meat, milk, oats, peanuts, peas, soy (soya) beans, sunflower seeds, tuna, walnuts |

| nutrient | benefits | rich food sources |
|---|---|---|
| Vitamin C (ascorbic acid) | Countless uses: promotes healthy blood capillaries and gums, and healthy skin and healing; aids absorption of iron and production of hemoglobin; boosts the body's defences against illnesses, helps protect against cancer, heart disease, allergies, infections, colds, stress and even aging. | Blackcurrants, broccoli, Brussels sprouts, grapefruit, green bell pepper, guava, kale, kiwi fruits, lemons, oranges, papayas, potatoes, spinach, strawberries, tomatoes, watercress |
| Vitamin D | Helps control use of calcium, needed for strong bones and teeth. | Cod liver oil, eggs, herring, mackerel, salmon, sardines |
| Vitamin E | Antioxidant; helps protect skin, circulation, brain, hormones and much more against effects of pollution; anti-clotting properties protect against heart disease. | Almonds, corn oil, hazelnuts, sunflower seeds and oil, walnuts, wheatgerm, wholewheat flour |
| Vitamin K | Needed to ensure the blood can clot normally. | Broccoli, Brussels sprouts, green cabbage, spinach, Camembert cheese, cauliflower, Cheddar cheese, green tea, oats, soy (soya) beans |
| **minerals** | | |
| Calcium | Best-known for building healthy bones, so particularly important for growing children and women reaching menopause at risk of osteoporosis. Also needed for muscles to contract and relax properly (including the heart muscle) and for healthy nerve function. | Almonds, Brazil nuts, cheese, green leafy vegetables, kelp, milk, molasses, salmon (canned), sardines (canned), sesame seeds, shrimp, soy (soya) beans, yogurt |
| Chromium | Helps processing of sugars and carbohydrates; works with the hormone insulin to balance blood sugar levels and hence, energy, concentration and appetite. | Beef, brewer's yeast, cheese, chicken, eggs, fish, fruit, liver, molasses, potatoes, seafood, whole grains |
| Copper | Needed in tiny amounts in the body for proper transport and production of red blood cells, and for triggering the release of iron to form hemoglobin. | Barley, cocoa, honey, lentils, molasses, mushrooms, mussels, nuts, oats, oysters, salmon, seeds, wheatgerm |
| Iodine | Forms part of the thyroid hormone that controls metabolism. | Cod liver oil, fish, oysters, table salt (iodized), seaweed, sunflower seeds |
| Iron | Part of hemoglobin – the red blood cell substance which carries oxygen from the lungs around the body to all the cells. Also needed as a catalyst for other processes in the body including cell reproduction. | Cashew nuts, cheese, egg yolks, chickpeas, green leafy vegetables, lean meat, lentils, molasses, mussels, offal, pumpkin seeds, sardines, seaweed, walnuts, wheatgerm |
| Magnesium | Works with calcium in many body functions, such as the transmission of messages down nerve cells, contraction and relaxation of muscles, growth and development of bones; also for the production of energy. | Almonds, fish, green leafy vegetables, molasses, nuts, soy (soya) beans, sesame and sunflower seeds, wheatgerm |

| nutrient | benefits | rich food sources |
|---|---|---|
| Manganese | An antioxidant, needed for healthy nerves and brain, and sex hormone production. | Avocados, barley, blackberries, brown rice, buckwheat, chestnuts, ginger, hazelnuts, oats, peas, pecans, seaweed, spinach |
| Potassium | Works with sodium to control normal nerve function and muscle contraction, including a regular heartbeat. The two also help balance the flow of water and nutrients in and out of cells preventing water retention. | Avocados, bananas, citrus fruits, lentils, milk, molasses, nuts, parsnips, potatoes, raisins, sardines (canned), spinach, whole grains |
| Selenium | Works with vitamin E as a powerful antioxidant to protect against degenerative diseases including certain cancers, heart disease and aging. | Avocados, broccoli, cabbage, celery, chicken, egg yolks, garlic, lentils, liver, milk, mushrooms, onions, seafood, wheatgerm, whole grains |
| Sodium | Alongside potassium, helps control the water balance in the body. Important for regulating blood pressure, healthy nervous function and normal muscle contraction and relaxation. | Table salt and most commercially processed and packaged foods, as well as bacon, bread, butter, ham, milk, canned vegetables |
| Sulphur | Antioxidant; also helps the liver release bile and detoxify various substances; needed for the production of collagen, our cellular "glue", so it is important for skin health and the repair of injured skin. | Cabbage, clams, eggs, fish, garlic, milk, onions, wheatgerm |
| Zinc | Acts as an antioxidant; is needed for normal taste; also needed for the growth and regeneration of new cells (particularly important in fetal development and teenagers); helps skin heal; needed for healthy reproductive organs, especially in men. | Egg yolks, fish, milk, molasses, oysters, peanuts, red meat, sesame seeds, soy (soya) beans, sunflower seeds, turkey, wheatgerm, whole grains |
| **other important nutrients** | | |
| Essential fatty acids | Needed for brain power, healthy nerves, smooth skin, hormone balance and more, these fats are incorporated into the membrane or skin of every cell in the body to keep each one working optimally. | Fish such as herring, mackerel, salmon and sardines; nuts; seeds such as hemp, flaxseeds, pumpkin, sesame and sunflower |
| Protein | Forms the basic material of all living cells – not just thoses that form the structure of our bodies but also blood cells, hormones and much more. Dietary sources are essential for rebuilding and regeneration, and for all body systems to function. | Eggs, fish, meat, milk, poultry, soy (soya) |

# juices for ailments

This chart lists the best foods to eat to help your body fight a range of common ailments, and offers a selection of the juice recipes that are rich in such foods. However, drinking the juices suggested is intended as a supplement to, and not a replacement for, professional medical advice.

| ailment | foods to eat | no. | juice title |
|---|---|---|---|
| Acne | All greens (such as broccoli, kale, parsley, spinach, watercress), fruit and vegetable fibre, garlic, seeds and their oils, yogurt | 172<br>175<br>257<br>310 | Green Waldorf<br>Super Defender<br>Heaven Scent<br>Purple Pineapple |
| Anemia | All greens (such as broccoli, kale, parsley, spinach, watercress), beets (beetroot), berries, kiwi fruit, citrus fruit, molasses | 176<br>189<br>180<br>066 | Grape & Green<br>Tabouleh<br>Beetles<br>Blackcurrant Twist |
| Angina | Broccoli, citrus fruis, fruit and vegetable fibre, kale, kiwi fruit, seeds and their oils, strawberries, watercress, wheatgerm | 169<br>172<br>245<br>258 | Green 'n' Pear It<br>Green Waldorf<br>Mango Blues<br>Globe Trotter |
| Arthritis | Apricots, berries; broccoli, carrots, garlic, ginger, kiwi fruit, mango, pineapple, red bell pepper, seeds and their oils, watercress, wheatgerm | 111<br>127<br>156<br>082 | Breakfast Pear<br>Joint Aid<br>Carrot Joint Aid<br>Berry Bonanza |
| Asthma | Apricots, berries, broccoli, carrots, ginger, kale, mango, melon, red bell pepper, seeds and their oils, sweet potato, watercress, watermelon | 120<br>177<br>135<br>261 | Ginger Zinger<br>Creamy Green<br>Carrot Crunch<br>Peachy Strawbs |
| Bladder problems | Blueberries, broccoli, citrus fruit, cranberries, garlic, kiwi fruit, strawberries, watermelon, yogurt | 028<br>137<br>267<br>276 | Cranapple<br>Carotene Catapult<br>Cranapple Crush<br>Watermelon Crush |
| Boils | All greens (such as broccoli, kale, parsley, spinach, watercress), berries, citrus fruits, fruit and vegetable fibre, garlic, kiwi fruits | 071<br>168<br>134<br>242 | Orange Pepper<br>Green Apple<br>Carrot Deep Cleanser<br>Summer Mango Special |
| Bronchitis | Apricots, broccoli, carrots, citrus fruit, garlic, kale, kiwi fruit, mango, melon, red bell pepper, seeds and their oils, strawberries, sweet potato, watercress, watermelons | 039<br>117<br>141<br>137 | Greatfruit C<br>Black Pineapple<br>Cold War<br>Carotene Catapult |
| Burns, cuts & bruises | Apricots, broccoli, cabbage, carrots, citrus fruit, garlic, kale, kiwi fruit, mango, milk, red bell pepper, seeds and their oils, strawberries, watercress, yogurt | 054<br>065<br>259<br>295 | Bright Orange<br>Muddy Puddle<br>Supreme Strawberry<br>Pinky Mango |
| Bursitis | Apricots, broccoli, cabbage, carrots, citrus fruit, garlic, ginger, kale, kiwi fruit, mango, pineapple, red bell pepper, seeds and their oils, strawberries, watercress | 120<br>127<br>078<br>262 | Ginger Zinger<br>Joint Aid<br>Sharp Citrusberry<br>Pink Berry Crush |
| Candidiasis | All greens (such as broccoli, kale, parsley, spinach, watercress), yogurt | 169<br>134<br>140<br><br>312 | Green 'n' Pear It<br>Carrot Deep Cleanser<br>Veggie Carotene Catapult<br>Pure Pineapple Creamy |

| ailment | foods to eat | no. | juice title |
|---|---|---|---|
| Cardiovascular disease | Broccoli, citrus fruit, fruit and vegetable fibre, kale, kiwi fruit, seeds and their oils, strawberries, watercress, wheatgerm | 057<br>127<br>217<br>259 | Power Packed C<br>Joint Aid<br>Take Heart<br>Supreme Strawberry |
| Chronic catarrh | Apricots, berries, carrots, citrus fruit, mango, melon, papaya, pineapple, watermelon | 136<br>149<br>117<br>257 | Carrot Digestif<br>Florida Carrot<br>Black Pineapple<br>Heaven Scent |
| Chronic fatigue | All greens (such as broccoli, kale, parsley, spinach, watercress), bananas, berries, citrus fruit, kale, kiwi fruit, seeds and their oils, watercress, wheatgerm, yogurt | 164<br>167<br>285<br>306 | Salad Cooler<br>Green Goddess<br>Green Banana Creamy<br>Purple Rain |
| Cold sores | Apricots, berries, broccoli, carrots, citrus fruit, garlic, kale, kiwi fruit, mango, red bell pepper, strawberries, tomatoes, watercress | 057<br>141<br>140<br>194 | Power Packed C<br>Cold War<br>Veggie Carotene Catapult<br>Green Tomatoes |
| Colitis | Apples, apricots, broccoli, cabbage, carrots, citrus fruit, fruit and vegetable fibre, kale, kiwi fruit, mango, melon, papaya, pineapple, seeds and seed oils, strawberries, watercress, wheatgerm | 012<br>140<br>173<br>254 | Apple Cleanser<br>Veggie Carotene Catapult<br>Sweet Green Melon<br>Papaya Pure |
| Common cold & 'flu | Apricots, broccoli, carrots, citrus fruit, garlic, ginger, kale, kiwi fruit, mango, melon, nectarines, red bell pepper, strawberries, watercress, watermelons | 057<br>141<br>244<br>263 | Power Packed C<br>Cold War<br>Nectargo<br>Citrus Strawbs |
| Constipation | Fruit and vegetable fibre, plenty of water and juices, seeds and their oils | 002<br>180<br>235<br>320 | Apple Basic<br>Beetles<br>Regular Banana<br>Apricot Regular |
| Cough | Apricots, berries, broccoli, carrots, citrus fruit, garlic, ginger, kale, kiwi fruit, mango, melon, papaya, pineapple, red bell pepper, sweet potato, watercress, watermelon | 040<br>117<br>137<br>255 | Surprising Sweetie<br>Black Pineapple<br>Carotene Catapult<br>Papaya Salad |
| Cystitis | Broccoli, citrus fruit, cranberries, garlic, kiwi fruit, strawberries, pineapple, watermelon, yogurt | 028<br>267<br>276<br>315 | Cranapple<br>Cranapple Crush<br>Watermelon Crush<br>Pinkypine |
| Dermatitis | Apples, apricots, berries, broccoli, carrots, celery, citrus fruit, garlic, kale, kiwi fruit, mango, melon, red bell pepper, seeds and their oils, watercress, watermelon | 022<br>133<br>205 | Apple Gone Loupey<br>Carrot Cleanser<br>Creamy Crunch<br>Any juice/smoothie with added seed oil |
| Diabetes | All greens (such as broccoli, kale, parsley, spinach, watercress), fruit and vegetable fibre, seeds and their oils | 136<br>176<br>175<br>252 | Carrot Digestif<br>Grape & Green<br>Super Defender<br>Pineberry |

| ailment | foods to eat | no. | juice title |
|---------|--------------|-----|-------------|
| Diarrhea | Apples, carrots, celery, pears | 001 | Eve's Downfall |
| | | 027 | Apple Zing |
| | | 100 | Pear Basic |
| | | 205 | Creamy Crunch |
| Diverticulitis | Fruit and vegetable fibre, garlic, ginger, yogurt | 004 | Basic with a Boost |
| | | 126 | Digestaid |
| | | 258 | Globe Trotter |
| | | 312 | Pure Pineapple Creamy |
| Dry skin | Apricots, berries, broccoli, carrots, citrus fruit, garlic, kale, kiwi fruit, mango, melon, red bell pepper, seeds and their oils, watercress, watermelon | 149 | Florida Carrot |
| | | 082 | Berry Bonanza |
| | | | Any juice/smoothie with added seeds/seed oil |
| Ear infection | Apricots, berries, broccoli, carrots, citrus fruit, garlic, kale, kiwi fruit, mango, melon, red bell pepper, seeds and their oils, watercress, watermelon | 070 | Water Cooler II |
| | | 141 | Cold War |
| | | 140 | Veggie Carotene Catapult |
| | | 082 | Berry Bonanza |
| Eczema | Berries, broccoli, carrots, garlic, kale, kiwi fruit, mango, melon, red bell pepper, seeds and their oils, watercress, watermelon | 127 | Joint Aid |
| | | 137 | Carotene Catapult |
| | | 177 | Creamy Green |
| | | 265 | Blue Healer |
| Endometriosis | All fruit and vegetable juice and fibre, seeds and their oils, soy (soya) milk, yogurt | 069 | Orange Aniseed Twist |
| | | 133 | Carrot Cleanser |
| | | 253 | Apple Squared |
| | | | Any smoothie with soy (soya) milk |
| Eyesight Problems | Apricots, berries, carrots, kale, mango, melon, pineapple, red bell pepper, watercress, watermelon | 129 | What's Up Doc? |
| | | 155 | Capple and Black |
| | | 265 | Blue Healer |
| | | 314 | Blue Pine Creamy |
| Fatigue | All fruit and vegetable juice and fibre, bananas, berries, carrots, pears, molasses, yogurt | 111 | Breakfast Pear |
| | | 133 | Carrot Cleanser |
| | | 285 | Green Banana Creamy |
| | | 307 | Mighty Berry |
| Fever | All fresh fruit and vegetable juices (especially apricots, berries, broccoli, carrots, citrus fruit, kale, kiwi fruit, mango, melon, red bell pepper, sweet potato, watercress, watermelon), garlic, seeds and their oils | 059 | Orange Medley |
| | | 141 | Cold War |
| | | 185 | Carotene Kick |
| | | 275 | Pure Watermelon |
| Fibroids | All greens (such as broccoli, kale, parsley, spinach, watercress), celery, citrus fruit, fennel, fruit and vegetable fibre, pears, soy (soya) milk, seeds and their oils | 069 | Orange Aniseed Twist |
| | | 169 | Green 'n' Pear It |
| | | | Any smoothie with soya milk and seeds/seed oil |
| Food poisoning | Apples, carrots, celery, ginger, pears | 002 | Apple Basic |
| | | 027 | Apple Zing |
| | | 100 | Pear Basic |
| | | 205 | Creamy Crunch |

| ailment | foods to eat | no. | juice title |
|---|---|---|---|
| Fractures | All greens (such as broccoli, kale, parsley, spinach, watercress), milk, molasses, peaches, pineapple, seeds and their oils, soy (soya) milk, yogurt | 065 | Muddy Puddle |
| | | 167 | Green Goddess |
| | | 290 | Peachy Banana Dream |
| | | 314 | Creamy Blue Pine |
| Gallbladder disorders | Apples, beet (beetroot), grapefruit, yogurt | 133 | Carrot Cleanser |
| | | 180 | Beetles |
| | | 181 | Blood 'n' Grape |
| | | 166 | Bloody Cuke |
| Gout | Cabbage, carrots, celery, cherries, kale, strawberries | 094 | Cherry Pie |
| | | 098 | Cherry Cooler |
| | | 145 | Carrot Lift |
| | | 214 | Soft and Sharp |
| Hemorrhoids | Apricots, berries, broccoli, carrots, citrus fruit, fruit and vegetable fibre, kale, kiwi fruit, mango, melon, red bell pepper, watercress, watermelon, wheatgerm | 016 | Black Orchard Berry Buster |
| | | 055 | Florida Blue |
| | | 155 | Capple and Black |
| | | 250 | Pastel Perfect |
| Hangovers | All greens (such as broccoli, kale, parsley, spinach, watercress), apples, bananas, carrots, celery, ginger, yogurt | 027 | Apple Zing |
| | | 133 | Carrot Cleanser |
| | | 277 | Creamy Cooler |
| | | 285 | Green Banana Creamy |
| Hay fever | Apricots, berries, broccoli, carrots, citrus fruit, kale, kiwi fruit, mango, melon, seeds and their oils, strawberries, sweet potato, watercress, watermelon | 057 | Power Packed C |
| | | 171 | Green Grapefruit |
| | | 137 | Carotene Catapult |
| | | 259 | Supreme Strawberry |
| Heartburn | Cabbage, papaya, pineapple | 030 | Bellyful |
| | | 113 | Gut Soother |
| | | 126 | Digestaid |
| | | 254 | Papaya Pure |
| Herpes | Berries, broccoli, carrots, citrus fruit, garlic, kale, kiwi fruit, seeds and their oils, tomatoes, watercress | 057 | Power Packed C |
| | | 141 | Cold War |
| | | 140 | Veggie Carotene Catapult |
| | | 194 | Green Tomatoes |
| High blood pressure | All fresh fruit and vegetables, especially greens (such as broccoli, kale, parsley, spinach, watercress), apples, garlic, seeds and their oils, wheatgerm | 022 | Apple Gone Loupey |
| | | 147 | Green Hit |
| | | 214 | Soft and Sharp |
| | | 217 | Take Heart |
| Hives (Urticaria) | Apricots, berries, broccoli, carrots, citrus fruit, garlic, kale, kiwi fruit, mango, melons, red bell pepper, sweet potato, watercress, watermelon | 057 | Power Packed C |
| | | 077 | Citrusberry |
| | | 185 | Carotene Kick |
| | | 294 | Pango Mango |
| Hypoglycemia | All fresh fruit and vegetable juice and fibre, cucumber, mango, seeds and their oils, yogurt | 176 | Grape & Green |
| | | 159 | Cucumber Refresher |
| | | 298 | Berry Mango |
| | | 306 | Purple Rain |
| Indigestion | Cabbage, papaya, pineapple | 030 | Bellyful |
| | | 113 | Gut Soother |
| | | 126 | Digestaid |
| | | 359 | Middle East Ginger |

| ailment | foods to eat | no. | juice title |
|---------|--------------|-----|-------------|
| Irritable bowel syndrome | All fruit and vegetable juice and fibre, all greens (such as broccoli, kale, parsley, spinach, watercress), bananas, cabbage, papaya, pineapple | 172<br>113<br>254<br>285 | Green Waldorf<br>Gut Soother<br>Papaya Pure<br>Green Banana Creamy |
| Kidney problems | All greens (such as broccoli, kale, parsley, spinach, watercress), apricots, carrots, celery, cranberries, cucumber, melon, molasses, pears, pumpkin, red bell pepper, sweet potato, watermelon | 105<br>210<br>162<br>167 | Pink Pear II<br>Pink Punch<br>Water Water Everywhere<br>Green Goddess |
| Memory problems | Fresh fruit and vegetable juices, especially berries, broccoli, citrus fruit, kale, kiwi fruit, watercress; seeds and their oils, wheatgerm | 063<br>172<br>245 | Orange Winter Crumble<br>Green Waldorf<br>Mango Blues<br>Any smoothie with seeds/seed oil |
| Menopause-related problems | All fruit and vegetable juice and fibre, apples, celery, fennel, garlic, soy (soya), seeds and their oils, wheatgerm | 012<br>069<br>209 | Apple Cleanser<br>Orange Aniseed Twist<br>Crunch Morning Favourite<br>Any smoothie with soy (soya) milk |
| Menstrual problems | All fruit and vegetable juice and fibre, beets, celery, fennel, garlic, seeds and their oils, soy (soya) | 069<br>175<br>179 | Orange Aniseed Twist<br>Super Defender<br>Beet Basic<br>Any smoothie with soy (soya) milk |
| Motion sickness | Cabbage, carrots, ginger, peppermint | 135<br>136<br>362<br>358 | Carrot Crunch<br>Carrot Digestif<br>Mint & Honey<br>Ginger Brew |
| Muscle cramps | All greens (such as broccoli, kale, parsley, spinach, watercress), molasses, seeds and their oils, wheatgerm | 012<br>150<br>207<br>167 | Apple Cleanser<br>Chlorophyll Carrot<br>Savoury Fruit<br>Green Goddess |
| Obesity | All fruit and vegetable juice and fibre | 019<br>133<br>209<br>248 | Waldorf Salad<br>Carrot Cleanser<br>Crunch Morning Favourite<br>Pineapple Zing |
| Osteoporosis prevention | All greens (such as broccoli, kale, parsley, spinach, watercress), garlic, milk, molasses, peaches, seeds and their oils, soy (soya) milk, yogurt | 125<br>169<br>172<br>318 | Green Pines<br>Green 'n' Pear It<br>Green Waldorf<br>Peachy Passion |
| Premenstrual syndrome | All greens (such as broccoli, kale, parsley, spinach, watercress), celery, fennel, garlic, seeds and their oils, soy (soya) | 067<br>169<br>172 | Muddy Tonic<br>Green 'n' Pear It<br>Green Waldorf<br>Any smoothie with soy (soya) milk |
| Prostate problems | Celery, fennel, fruit and vegetable fibre, garlic, molasses, soy (soya), seeds and their oils, tomatoes | 188<br>203<br>172<br>283 | Ginger Tom<br>Tomorange<br>Green Waldorf<br>Creamy Black Banana |

| ailment | foods to eat | no. | juice title |
|---|---|---|---|
| Psoriasis | Apricots, broccoli, carrots, fruit and vegetable fibre, mango, pumpkin, red bell pepper, seeds and their oils, sweet potato, watercress | 120 | Ginger Zinger |
| | | 137 | Carotene Catapult |
| | | 177 | Creamy Green |
| | | 244 | Nectargo |
| Shingles | Apricots, berries, broccoli, carrots, citrus fruit, garlic, kale, kiwi fruit, mango, melon, red bell pepper, sweet potato, seeds and their oils, watercress, watermelon | 057 | Power Packed C |
| | | 141 | Cold War |
| | | 137 | Carotene Catapult |
| | | 175 | Super Defender |
| Sinusitis | Apricots, berries, broccoli, carrots, citrus fruit, kale, kiwi fruit, mango, melon, red bell pepper, sweet potato, seeds and their oils, watercress, watermelon | 117 | Black Pineapple |
| | | 141 | Cold War |
| | | 177 | Creamy Green |
| | | 265 | Blue Healer |
| Sleeping problems | All greens (such as broccoli, kale, parsley, spinach, watercress), apples, bananas, milk, molasses, seeds, soy (soya) milk, yogurt | 024 | Apple Lullaby |
| | | 174 | Green Lullaby |
| | | 282 | Creamy Bananacot |
| | | 289 | Banana Heaven |
| Sprains, strains & other injuries | All greens (such as broccoli, kale, parsley, spinach, watercress), garlic, milk, molasses, seeds and their oils, soy (soya) milk, yogurt | 030 | Bellyful |
| | | 065 | Muddy Puddle |
| | | 167 | Green Goddess |
| | | 285 | Creamy Green Banana |
| Stomach ulcers | Cabbage, carrots, melon, papaya | 030 | Bellyful |
| | | 136 | Carrot Digestif |
| | | 173 | Sweet Green Melon |
| | | 254 | Papaya Pure |
| Stress | All fruit and vegetable juice and fibre, all greens (such as broccoli, kale, parsley, spinach, watercress), berries, carrots, citrus fruit, milk, molasses, pineapple, red bell pepper, seeds and their oils, soy (soya) milk, wheatgerm, yogurt | 133 | Carrot Cleanser |
| | | 172 | Green Waldorf |
| | | 285 | Creamy Green Banana |
| | | 315 | Pinkypine |
| Sunburn | Apricots, berries (especially blackcurrants), broccoli, carrots, citrus fruit, garlic, kiwi fruit, mango, pumpkin, red bell pepper, strawberries, sweet potatoes, watercress | 062 | Bitter Melon |
| | | 002 | Apple Basic |
| | | 277 | Creamy Cooler |
| | | 279 | Green Sensation |
| Tonsillitis | Apricots, berries, broccoli, carrots, citrus fruit, garlic, kale, kiwi fruit, mango, melon, pineapple, red bell pepper, seeds and their oils, sweet potato, watercress, watermelon | 117 | Black Pineapple |
| | | 116 | Pink Pineapple |
| | | 141 | Cold War |
| | | 265 | Blue Healer |
| Varicose veins | All fruit and vegetable juice and fibre, berries, broccoli, citrus fruit, kale, kiwi fruit, seeds and their oils, watercress, wheatgerm | 002 | Apple Basic |
| | | 055 | Florida Blue |
| | | 082 | Berry Bonanza |
| | | 320 | Apricot Regular |
| Water retention | Celery, cucumber, melon, watermelon | 206 | Cool 'n' Pale II |
| | | 161 | Mellow Melon |
| | | 213 | Salty Sharp Melon |
| | | 162 | Water Water Everywhere |

# Index

References are to page numbers, not recipes. This index should be used in conjuntion with the index of ailments on pp.182–7 and the suggested juice courses on pp.176–8.